HENRY FUSELI

Martin Myrone

British Artists

Tate Publishing

Front cover: *Percival Delivering Belisane from the Enchantment of Urma* 1783 (fig.37, detail)

Back cover: *The Shepherd's Dream, from 'Paradise Lost'* 1793 (fig.50, detail)

Frontispiece: *Self-Portrait as a Faun* (detail), pencil and chalk on paper, 32.2 × 42.7 (12⅝ × 16¾), Tate; purchased as part of the Oppé Collection with assistance from the National Lottery through the Heritage Lottery Fund 1996

Published by order of the Tate Trustees by
Tate Gallery Publishing Ltd
Millbank, London SW1P 4RG

© Tate Gallery Publishing Ltd 2001

The moral rights of the author have been asserted

ISBN 1 85437 357 9

A catalogue record for this book is available from the British Library

Cover design by Slatter-Anderson, London

Concept design James Shurmer
Book design Caroline Johnston

Printed in Hong Kong by South Seas International Press Ltd

Measurements are given in centimetres, height before width, followed by inches in brackets

CONTENTS

INTRODUCTION
'BOTH TURK AND JEW'

As the painter of some of the most imaginative, dramatic and ferociously sexual imagery in British art, the Swiss-born Henry Fuseli (1741–1825) has fascinated and appalled in equal measures since he first emerged as a public figure in the 1770s. In a career that lasted over half a century, through one of the most turbulent periods of British culture and society, he achieved enormous fame and notoriety as an artist, teacher and writer. In the nineteenth century, his art may have gradually fallen into obscurity, but he was still remembered as one of the great eccentric personalities of an age of great personalities. Although hardly a household name today, his images are among the most familiar in the history of art. *The Nightmare* in particular is instantly recognisable, reproduced in publications literary, scholarly and popular as an icon of irrational eroticism (fig.1). His famous drawing known as *The Artist in Despair over the Magnitude of Antique Fragments* has been almost mandatory as a textbook illustration of late eighteenth-century attitudes towards the classical past (fig.2). More generally, his vividly stylised images of ghosts and fairies, muscle-bound superheroes, fainting maidens and voracious viragos are obvious prototypes for the figures in today's comic-books, action movies and computer games (fig.3).

Like modern-day fantasy images, Fuseli's art can at its best have an engaging dynamism. Similarly, it can appear crass and sensationalist. The uneven and contradictory qualities of his work have always been recognised. For his contemporaries, Fuseli was by turns the greatest artist in Britain, and quite possibly the greatest artist since Michelangelo, or an artistic deviant intent on demolishing the finest traditions of painting, who was figuratively, and for some commentators even literally, driven mad by his consumption of raw pork or opium. Fuseli himself was full of apparent contradictions, condemning formal art education while spending more than twenty years as a teacher at the Royal Academy of Art, abusive and vulgar in his behaviour while proclaiming his intellectual refinement, and damning public taste while also addressing a broad market. It was the very contrariness and oddness of Fuseli as an artist and as a character that stimulated modern interest in him. Significantly, the revival of interest in Fuseli dates to the 1930s and 1940s, when the concern with the supernatural and irrational aspects of his art was tied to the widening appeal of Surrealism. As Ruthven Todd wrote in 1946, a revived appreciation of Fuseli's imagery was perhaps only a natural extension of the predilection for 'the desolate arcades and squares of Chirico, the plasmic dancing amoeba of [Joán] Miró and the flexible watches, the crutch-supported buttocks and the hidden images of Salvador Dali'.[1] More recent art histories have continued to stress the individualistic and aberrant character of

1 *The Nightmare*
1781
Oil on canvas
101 × 127
(39⅜ × 50)
Detroit Institute of
Arts, Detroit;
Founders Society
Purchase with funds
from Mr and Mrs
Bert L. Smokler and
Mr and Mrs
Lawrence A.
Fleischman

2 *The Artist in
Despair over the
Magnitude of Antique
Fragments* 1778–80
Pen and wash
drawing
42 × 35.3
(16½ × 13⅞)
Kunsthaus Zurich

his work, which confounds conventional art-historical classification. He has been located as, variously, a Romantic, a Neoclassicist, a 'Romantic Classicist', purveyor of the 'Neoclassic horrific' or 'Sado-Mannerist', and the subtlest interpreter of Fuseli's writings on art has stressed the presence of 'a complex irony' in his thinking, which often seems self-contradictory.[2] Although the style and content of his imagery has been studied intensively, and although various proposals have been made with regard to the psychological basis of his art, he remains characterised by contradiction. Fuseli is still, as his friend William Blake quipped, 'both Turk and Jew', something of an enigma.[3]

This book offers a new interpretation of Fuseli, one that places the artist firmly within his time. It does not attempt to see through the myth-making and contradictions, but rather takes them as central factors in the way his art functioned historically. It argues that Fuseli's individualism was not the consequence of any personal, psychological traits – nor even of a sweeping cultural transition from Neoclassicism to Romanticism – but the product of a very specific cultural moment, showing, in particular, how new forms of publicity conditioned his art. Fuseli needs to be understood as, in a recognisably modern sense, a media phenomenon. He made great claims for himself, as an artist, an intellectual, and above all as a wild genius whose imagination roamed in places conventional society could not imagine. In one way or another, many of his peers grew to believe him. But his claims would have meant nothing if it were not for the fact that at that precise moment, all those things were expected, demanded even, and that new institutional and critical structures emerged that could give them credence. Fuseli was the kind of artist that many people wanted to believe in. The following chapters look at his art in this context, focusing on the works he created for public show and on the period of his greatest innovation, from the 1770s to around 1800. In Chapter 1, the exaggerated stylisation that characterised his art is related to the intensely competitive international art community of Rome in the 1770s. Chapter 2 sets his continuing innovations of style and subject against the novel modes of looking at and talking about art that emerged in London's public exhibitions. Chapter 3 looks at the ways his idiosyncrasies were accommodated to ideals of the British School of art that were being promoted by officialdom and commercial entrepreneurs, while the final chapter briefly considers his reputation and influence. Throughout, a recurring theme is the way Fuseli's self-proclaimed genius was a response to and a contribution towards a rapid overhaul of the way art was produced and consumed, which helped lay the foundations of the modern art world.

When Fuseli first arrived in London in 1764, it was already clear that the art scene was entering a period of radical change. A mere five years earlier, there were no regular art exhibitions, very little in the way of art criticism, and only an informal system of art education. There was nothing that could be described as a 'public' for art. For those not wealthy enough to own their own pictures and display them in their own galleries, art was something seen occasionally in shop windows and in salerooms, or as decoration in public buildings. Moreover, the modern British art that was available was not generally of a kind conventionally considered as high art. What patronage there

3 *Satan Starts from
the Touch of Ithuriel's
Spear* 1776
Pen and wash
drawing
27.1 × 39.3
(10⅝ × 15⅛)
The National
Museum of Fine
Arts, Stockholm

was tended to be for portraiture and landscape paintings, rather than for history painting, that is, paintings on a large scale based on noble themes from
the Bible, important historical events or serious literature, traditionally
defined as the highest genre of art. But from the late 1750s there were increasingly articulate, and confident, moves to change this situation. In 1759 the
patriotic Society for the Encouragement of Arts, Manufactures and Commerce inaugurated a wide-ranging scheme of art competitions that offered
pecuniary awards for high-minded artists and helped establish the issue of
modern British history painting as a national concern. In 1760 the first
proper exhibition of modern British art was held, organised by the Society of
Artists. This became an annual event, joined from 1761 by a second exhibition
run by the rival Free Society of Artists. Meanwhile, the long-mooted plan to
establish a central, official art institution gained impetus, and the Royal Char-
ter bestowed on the Society of Artists in 1765 was followed, in 1768, by the
foundation of the Royal Academy, Britain's first official art school and exhibiting society. The proclaimed ambition of the Academy was to create a public
platform for the most ambitious kinds of art – what its first president, Sir
Joshua Reynolds, called the 'Great Style', history paintings based on the
exalted models of ancient Greek and Roman sculpture and the paintings of
Renaissance Italy. In the course of barely a decade, London acquired for the
first time practical organisations that promised to support contemporary
artists in their highest ambitions. Most significantly of all, history painting,
traditionally the preserve of an insular social elite, became the topic of much
more open public discussion. High art was thus caught up in a wider change
in British society, where the best claim to status and authority was shifting
from the old property-owning elite onto a broader public defined through
their participation in cultural activities – reading newspapers and books,
going to the theatre, looking at pictures. Fashion and taste, driven forward by

commercial enterprise, were thereby modulating an old hierarchy of wealth and inherited status.

Over the same period, ideas about art and culture were being overhauled just as thoroughly. The late 1750s and 1760s saw a remarkable acceleration in the discussion of aesthetics and artistic value, which were often openly critical of contemporary culture. A series of seminal publications were issued, in the fields of aesthetic philosophy, literature and art history. Edmund Burke's *Philosophical Enquiry into our Ideas of the Sublime and the Beautiful* (1757) proposed a dramatic division between the seductive, but ultimately enervating, ideal of the 'Beautiful', and the threatening, but ultimately energising, ideal of the 'Sublime', characterised by grandeur, obscurity and terror, which was to prove profoundly influential. Edward Young's *Conjectures on Original Composition* (1759) helped articulate a novel ideal of creative genius, founded not on the rules and regulations favoured by earlier generations, but on individualism and even social alienation. At the same time, the publication of James Macpherson's *Poems of Ossian* (1762–5), purporting to be a translation from an ancient Gaelic manuscript, signalled a new concern for the moral purity represented by primal forms of cultural expression, a tendency also apparent in the renewed interest in the antique. While not wishing to suggest that artistic practice should be interpreted as being 'influenced' by this upsurge of critical debate in any simple sense, the well-educated Fuseli was intently aware of these discussions, and they can certainly be seen as setting the stage for his own reformist artistic desires.

Considered individually, each of these changes is remarkable. Considered together, it is clear that the cultural environment was changing rapidly. We can be quite precise about the historical circumstances that stirred these changes. For the period 1756–63, Britain was engaged in the Seven Years War, the bloodiest war of the eighteenth century, and the first truly global, imperial war. In the early years of the conflict Britain seemed doomed to lose, producing a real sense of crisis that was blamed very explicitly on the moral and aesthetic corruption of modern Britons. The emergence of critical voices calling for practical and imaginative reform was part of a larger, highly politicised effort to change society from a variety of quarters, urged forward by the cataclysm of the war, and the ensuing, troubled expansion of the Empire. The rapid changes within the world of art from the late 1750s onwards can properly be interpreted as evidence of the ongoing friction between different social classes, each vying for the claim to cultural leadership: the old landed gentry, the newly powerful and articulate middle classes, an anonymous public for art in the act of emerging as a real market force, and the cultural producers themselves. Consequently, the role of art in society – the basic questions about what it should represent, how, and for whom – was very much in question. The most fascinating aspect of Fuseli's art is the way that it not only participated in these changes, but how in their very form and subject matter his images also represented the processes of change themselves. Ultimately, if Fuseli's art is strange, sensationalist, confused and sometimes plain silly, it may be that the new world of art it helped usher in had exactly those qualities.

1

'THE WILD PAINTER'

In May 1768, Henry Fuseli wrote to Johann Caspar Lavater, a friend since his student days in Zurich a decade before: 'How are things with me? Here is something for my self-regard. Reynolds tells me that I will be the greatest painter of the age, if I can only spend a few years in Rome.'[1]

Fuseli was then 37 years old, an ordained Zwinglian minister who had exiled himself from his native Switzerland following his part in a local political dispute, and who had since travelled in Germany before settling in London in 1764. Except for a handful of book illustrations, he had not publicly demonstrated any great ability as a visual artist. Since coming to England he had, however, made some name for himself as a translator and author. To date, his most notable publications were the translation from the German of J.J. Winckelmann's *Reflection on the Painting and Sculpture of the Greeks* (1765), the crucial polemical tract in the revival of classicism, and his own *Remarks on the Writings and Conduct of J.J. Rousseau* (1767). Neither was greeted with great acclaim or interest, although the latter, a rather eccentric and now almost wholly impenetrable philosophical tract emerging from the very public argument between the philosophers Jean Jacques Rousseau and David Hume, at least created a minor literary controversy. Published anonymously, the text was first attributed to Lawrence Sterne, author of *Tristram Shandy*, but the true identity of the author was no great secret: Hume himself discovered that it was 'one Fuseli, an Engraver'.[2]

Yet by 1768, Fuseli, picking up on what may have been only a passing remark by Sir Joshua Reynolds (famously reticent in his praise), had resolved that he was going to be the greatest artist of the age. The appearance of artistic aspirations was not entirely unwarranted or unexpected. Fuseli was born as Johann Heinrich Füssli into a family of artists with strong cultural roots in Zurich. His father, Johann Caspar Füssli the Elder was a well-established painter, civic official and art historian. While Fuseli's brothers and sisters became artists, Henry was for some reason directed by his father towards the priesthood. In what we may imagine was a typical piece of self-promotion, Fuseli told his biographer, John Knowles, that he continued to draw in secret, developing ambidexterity so that he could draw furtively with one hand while appearing to read with a book in the other (in fact, the evidence of Fuseli's drawings suggests a pretty constant left-handedness). The youthful drawings that survive focus on medieval battles, fanciful brigandry and the world of the Renaissance artist, inspired by and often copied directly from the elaborate and highly mannered imagery of sixteenth- and seventeenth-century Swiss artists (fig.4).

In accordance with his father's wishes, at the age of 18 Fuseli enrolled at

4 *Fool in a Fool's Cap Having his Portrait Painted by a Bespectacled Artist*
1757–9
Pen and wash drawing
30 × 20.9
(11⅞ × 8⅛)
Kunsthaus Zurich

the Caroline College in Zurich to study theology. At that time, the College was a thriving intellectual centre, mainly due to the presence of Johann Jakob Bodmer and Johann Jakob Breitinger. They were leading lights in German literature, spearheading a revolutionary approach to art that emphasised emotionalism and anti-rationalism. Fuseli was taught and befriended by both, and their passionate interest in the supposedly republican and liberal traditions of English culture, idealisation of creative genius and insistence on the role of sublime grandeur and fantasy were to prove decisive for him. Most of all, the reforming zeal that characterised Bodmer and Breitinger's views was echoed in Fuseli's later art and writings.

It was at the College that Fuseli met Lavater, a fellow student in theology, who later gained international fame for his writings on physiognomy. Taking their teachers' reforming instincts into the realm of local politics, they openly criticised the corrupt administration of a magistrate, Felix Grebel, in the winter of 1762. Though the case against Grebel was eventually proved, and he was disgraced, the controversy was such that they were advised to leave the area. They travelled together through Germany, studying with the mathematician and philosopher Johann Sulzer in Berlin and with the theologian Johann Joachim Spalding in Swedish Pomerania, before parting (providing Fuseli with the chance to write a rather overheated prose poem on the theme of friendship and loss). Fuseli went back to Berlin, where he assisted Sulzer and designed illustrations for Bodmer's epic poem on Noah (fig. 5), and worked on a German translation of Lady Mary Wortley Montagu's *Letters* (published in 1763). A plan was concocted between Sulzer and the English ambassador to the court of Frederick the Great, Sir Andrew Mitchell, to send Fuseli to London as a sort of cultural emissary.

Fuseli travelled to London with Mitchell in the spring of 1764, where he was quickly introduced to 'advanced' literary society, notably the publishers Andrew Millar and Joseph Johnson, with whom he lodged. He never formally fulfilled his role as a cultural go-between, and instead launched himself into the world of letters, clearly impressing with his combination of wide-ranging erudition, forthright, distinctly modern views and 'exotic' Germanic origins. He may have published some articles in 1764–5, but the first firm evidence of his literary work in England was his translation of Winckelmann. The German scholar's views on the supreme qualities of ancient art, notably its chasteness, calmness and expressive simplicity, held great sway over the artists and critics of the 1760s and 1770s. However, Fuseli's translation was not well received, and what purported to be a second edition of 1766 was in fact a ploy for getting rid of the leftover stock. Despite the publication of further articles and reviews, Fuseli was obliged to work as a travelling tutor to the

5 Christian Gottfried
Matthes after Henry
Fuseli
*Lamech Speaks to the
Spirit of Tydor on the
Purgatorial Moon*
1764
Etching published in
Johann Jakob
Bodmer, *Die Noachide*
(Berlin 1765)
12.9 × 9.5 (5 × 3¾)
The British Library
[1152.b.19]

6 Charles Grignion
after Henry Fuseli
*Justice and Liberty
Hanged, while Voltaire
Rides Monster
Humanity and Jean-
Jacques Rousseau
Takes his Measure*
1767
Engraved
frontispiece to Henry
Fuseli, *Remarks in the
Writings and Conduct
of J.J. Rousseau*
(London 1767)
13.2 × 8.5
(5¼ × 3⅜)
The British Library
[11826.aa.14]

teenage Lord Chewton, an appointment that ended disastrously in a punch-up. But the appointment at least provided the opportunity to travel to Paris, leading to a meeting with the Swiss philosopher Jean Jacques Rousseau, famed for his attacks on the corruption of contemporary society. It was after that meeting that Fuseli wrote his *Remarks on Rousseau*. While this, as noted, was little noticed by contemporaries (the positive reviews that did appear can all be traced to Fuseli's circle, and in one instance to Fuseli himself), modern scholars have reassessed its importance. At the time, Rousseau was often cari-catured as crudely proposing a 'return to nature' that would lead mankind back into a savage state. Most famously, Voltaire had sarcastically instructed Rousseau's followers to take his teachings to their logical end and go and eat the grass in Hyde Park. Fuseli, however, recognised that Rousseau's thinking was more subtle, and his frontispiece makes fun of Voltaire by showing him riding on the back of a 'savage' man, while Rousseau, in the bizarre Armen-ian peasant costume he affected, stands to one side holding the plumb-line of Truth (fig.6).

Winckelmann and Rousseau were among the most advanced thinkers of the day. In their different fields, both were concerned with the reform of mod-ern culture, and proposed a return to a truer state of human creativity. The effusive commentaries on the corruption of contemporary culture and the rarity of true genius found in Fuseli's published writings and letters of the 1760s testify to their influence, and to the continuing role of Bodmer and Breitinger in his thought. Their anxieties about the course of modern culture were especially relevant to a younger generation trying to make its way in the world of art and literature. With the privileges supplied by his family background and education, Fuseli could move relatively freely within the literary world of London. But his activities show that that world did not provide great security. The sum total of his output in the 1760s consisted of a few translations, some essays and reviews, some book illustration, and a failed attempt at literary reputation with the *Remarks*. His career to date could be described as scrappy, opportunistic and largely improvised. The continuing growth of middle-class literate society seemed to promise renewed liberties and the further erosion of elite privileges, but, necessarily functioning on commercial lines, it did not offer great certainty, either with regard to individual career paths or cultural values more generally. It was therefore no coincidence that the most influential writers and thinkers proposed (if only rhetorically) certainties – the certainties of an authentically emotive poetic voice, the supreme values of ancient art, the incontrovertible power of 'genius' and the 'sublime'.

Fuseli's art, and his persona as 'a gentleman, a scholar, a philosopher, a genius and a man of wit',[3] were concerned with precisely such certainties. His drawings of the later 1760s show a new preoccupation with the most dramatic and unusual subjects from English literature and theatre (which Fuseli admired to excess), continuing in the dense graphic style he had developed studying the Swiss old masters, with its stylised treatment of draperies and anatomy, and bizarrely manipulated spaces (fig.7). By the end of the 1760s a new confidence is evident in his work, displayed in his increasingly bold use of light and shade, surer draughtsmanship and the larger scale of his designs. During 1768 and 1769 Fuseli was active raising funds for his trip to Italy, and

7 Garrick as the Duke of Gloucester Waiting for Lady Anne at the Funeral Procession of her Father-in-Law, King Henry VI 1766 Pen and wash drawing 31.7 × 45.7 (12½ × 18) Kunsthaus Zurich

the works he executed then, including the large and elaborate print of *The Apparition Appears to Dion* (fig.8), were produced in an effort to secure backing for the journey. At the same time he continued his literary career by publishing more articles and preparing an ambitious history of German poetry. But this project was abandoned following a fire at Johnson's house in January 1770 that destroyed all his manuscripts. Shortly afterwards, Fuseli set out to Rome to study art, backed by a number of well-off middle-class professionals and businessmen, most importantly the banker Thomas Coutts. Given the fact that Fuseli had not really demonstrated his potential as an artist by any of the usual means – he had not studied under a painter, or at an art school, or attempted to make a living as an artist in the lucrative fields of portraiture or landscape – this was something of a coup. Coming from a highly educated, middle-class background, Fuseli was a rarity among artists of the day, securing him exceptional access to the cultural world of London. Significant also is the way Fuseli's drawings of those years conform so closely to the emerging literary ideals of the artist as socially alienated and individualist. With his thick accent (which, perforce, served to associate him with the 'savage' Rousseau) giving him an exotic, alien aura, Fuseli himself must also have fulfilled expectations of what a potential genius might be, as far as the advanced literary circles he associated with were concerned. His unremitting commitment to poetic subjects, often (as with the *Dion* print) of such a recondite nature that it required a highly educated viewer to decipher them, and always on dramatic, tragic and violent themes, signalled his ambitions unequivocally. In that respect, Fuseli's failure to conform to current standards of artistic practice could appear a virtue.

Fuseli's decision to travel to Italy in order to make himself 'the greatest painter of the age' was entirely predictable. Rome in the eighteenth century was the cultural capital of Europe, the home of the most admired masterpieces of ancient and modern art. The convention of the Grand Tour, the extended trip to the Continent (but particularly Italy) that young gentlemen were expected to undertake in order to complete their education before settling down at home, ensured that Rome was always busy with potential patrons and contacts. The leading lights of the British art world in the 1760s, including Reynolds, the landscape painter Richard Wilson, and the architects William Chambers and Robert Adam, had all spent extended periods in Rome, attracting commissions and 'networking'. For history painters especially, Italy appeared to offer opportunities still rarely encountered at home. Since 1759 the Scottish painter Gavin Hamilton had been engaged on a hugely ambitious series of canvases based on scenes from Homer's *Iliad*, painted for various members of the British social elite. His images combined a severe style derived from the traditions of classical art with emotionally charged themes calculated to appeal to the current taste for 'sentimental' subjects (fig.9). The aggressively marketed engravings reproducing these works ensured that Hamilton gained a wide reputation as the most forward-looking history painter of the day. Others, notably the American-born Benjamin West, followed his example. After studying in Italy in 1760–3, West had come to London and established himself as the leading painter of historical works on

8 *The Apparition Appears to Dion, Wielding a Broom*
1768
Hand-coloured etching
46 × 49
(18⅛ × 19¼)
The British Museum

Spectrum Dioneum

9 Gavin Hamilton
*Sketch for
'Andromache
Mourning the Death of
Hector'* c.1759
Oil on canvas
64.2 × 98.5
(25¼ × 38¾)
National Gallery of
Scotland

10 Benjamin West
*Pylades and Orestes
Brought as Victims
before Iphigenia* 1766
Oil on canvas
100.3 × 126.4
(39½ × 49¾)
Tate

classical themes (fig. 10). By the time Fuseli was preparing his own trip to Italy, West had secured patronage from some of the most important men in England, including George III.

The examples set by Hamilton and West encouraged a whole generation of younger British artists in their ambitions. Further bolstered by the optimism surrounding the foundation of the Royal Academy, scores travelled to Italy in pursuit of similar fame and fortune. In the event, Hamilton and West were to prove to be exceptional cases. The sheer weight of numbers meant that British artists who attempted to emulate them did not meet with a similar success. In practice, life for an artist in Rome was intensely competitive. The British community there became a hotbed of intrigue and scandal, as aspiring artists competed with each other for the patronage that was available.

Fuseli's response to these conditions was further to develop the idiosyncratic characteristics of his art, and even further to inflate the pretensions of his imagery to sublime grandeur. Art historians have seen the eight years Fuseli eventually spent in Rome as the formative period of his art, where, inspired by classical sculpture and by Michelangelo, he lost faith in the established aesthetic theories of quiet classicism promulgated by Winckelmann to formulate a radically new style. The drawings that survive from Fuseli's Roman period certainly demonstrate a restless graphic experimentation, as the linearity already apparent in his English drawings is refined into the most economical notational system. Although there are sketches that appear to be based on specific paintings and sculptures he could have seen in Rome, these are generally free interpretations, emphasising a sense of dynamic virility. His drawings after the gigantic ancient figures of the 'Horsetamers' (Piazza del

18

11 *Study after the
'Horsetamer' of
Phidias* 1770–5
Black crayon
drawing
26.7 × 18.9
(10½ × 7⅜)
Kunsthaus Zurich

Quirinale, Rome) are especially notable, exaggerating the muscular physique of the originals to the extreme, and providing Fuseli with a stock pose he was to use many times in his compositions (fig.11). But he was more occupied with producing invented compositions, based on the most exalted literary sources, including Shakespeare, Homer and Dante (fig.12). These demonstrate a dependence on a number of artistic models, above all Michelangelo, but also the mannerist artists who imitated and manipulated his style in the sixteenth and seventeenth centuries. Fuseli's use of pure line and simple, solid bands of washed tone to define form are, for instance, especially reminiscent of the work of Luca Cambiaso (fig.13), while elsewhere his elongated figures and agitated hatching recall the drawings of Baccio Bandinelli. Referring to these artistic models allowed Fuseli to cultivate the mannerisms already apparent in his draughtsmanship. It also served to identify him with artists always noted (though more rarely admired) for an excessive virtuosity that went beyond the norms established in the Renaissance. Fuseli's dynamically attenuated figures in their mould could function as almost hieroglyphic signs of artistic excess.

Fuseli was not alone in these preoccupations. A number of artists in Rome from the beginning of the 1770s were similarly exploring the expressive potential of mannerism, and comparably dramatic subjects, including the Scottish

12 *Dante and Virgil
on the Ice of Cocytus*
1774
Pen and wash
drawing
39 × 27.4
(15⅜ × 10¾)
Kunsthaus Zurich

painter Alexander Runciman (fig.14), the English artists Thomas Banks, George Romney and James Jefferys, the Swedish sculptor Johan Tobias Sergel and the Danish painter Nicolas Abildgaard – all sometimes identified as members of a 'Fuseli circle'.[4] What held them together was the heady social life of the artistic community in Rome (encompassing a variety of sexual adventures) and, more cerebrally, a common agenda based on the need to rejuvenate modern art through primal, virile expressionism. These were artists

13 Luca Cambiaso
*Dante and Virgil in the
Infernal Region*
Pen, bistre and wash
drawing
19.4 × 24.6
(7⅝ × 9⅝)
The Courtauld
Institute Gallery,
London

14 Alexander
Runciman
The Death of Oscar
1772
Pen and wash
drawing
34.3 × 49.2
(13½ × 19⅜)
National Gallery of
Scotland

working closely together but also in competition with each other to forge the more expressive and individual style. One of the older, and certainly more educated, members of this group, Fuseli was recognised as its leading figure, and his compositions were even copied faithfully by the younger British artists, Prince Hoare and James Northcote (fig.15). He was seen as the fulfilment of the modern ideal of the creative genius, infused with potent energy (even in the literally sexual sense). He was, as contemporaries reported, the 'wild painter', the 'greatest figure' in Rome, who was 'in everything, extreme'.[5] Writing to Johann Gottfried Herder, Fuseli's old friend Lavater enthusiastically described him as:

> the most original genius I know. Nothing but energy, profusion and
> calm! the wildness of the warrior – and the feeling of supreme
> sublimity! But inexorable to all pleadings – and yet led as easily as a
> child by looks and hints, which he greatly feels! His spirits are storm-
> wind, his ministers flames of fire! He goes upon the wings of the wind.
> His laughter is the mockery of hell and his love – a deadly lightning-
> flash.[6]

Fuseli himself was happy to concur with such a view. In a quite spectacularly overwrought '2nd Ode on Art', he haughtily dismissed the academic artists from around Europe, the 'vermin of art' who were 'blown by the winds' to Rome, while he professed his true understanding of the 'beauty and majesty' of Michelangelo's Sistine Chapel decorations.[7] This is the image of Fuseli as the artist isolated by his genius, and caught up in the whirlwind of his emotions, conjured by the po-faced portrait by Northcote painted at the end of his stay in Rome (fig.16). It is also the image comically deflated in a caricature

15 James Northcote after Henry Fuseli *Galanthis Deceives Eleithyia by Announcing the Birth of Hercules c.*1777–8 Pen and wash drawing 31.6 × 42.8 (12½ × 16⅞) The Courtauld Institute Gallery, London

16 James Northcote
*Portrait of Henry
Fuseli* 1778
Oil on canvas
77 × 64
(30⅜ × 25¼)
National Portrait
Gallery, London

17 Johan Tobias
Sergel
*Caricature of Henry
Fuseli* 1770–8
Pen and wash
drawing
23.4 × 19.4
(9¼ × 7⅝)
The National
Museum of Fine
Arts, Stockholm

drawing by his close friend Sergel, showing the painter assailed by lightning bolts shooting from the backsides of the Muses (fig.17). Yet even such jesting only further helped to bolster Fuseli's reputation as a uniquely eccentric and original genius.

It would be a mistake, however, to take these comments at face value, and imagine Fuseli in glorious isolation grappling with the examples of classical sculpture and Michelangelo in a struggle to define his own artistic genius. He took an active part in the social life of the Grand Tour, associating with such eminent figures as the famous musicologist Charles Burney and the fabulously wealthy historian William Beckford, ingratiating himself with the art dealer James Byres, and perhaps even acting as a *cicerone* (tourist guide). And although almost all the surviving works from his Roman period are drawings, often unfinished, there is evidence that he acquired considerable employment as a painter. In 1773 it was reported that he had turned down a commission for 1,500 guineas to copy 'a capital picture'.[8] A year later the sculptor Thomas Banks stated that 'he had pictures bespoke to the amount of £1300' and an English Jesuit in Rome, Father Thorpe, recorded that Fuseli was 'painting scenes from Shakespear in figures as large as life'.[9] These may be the '16 Shakespeare pieces' that the artist mentioned as sold for the not inconsiderable sum of 8,000 florins (about £960) in a letter to Lavater.[10] With the extra money begged or borrowed from his old friends in London and Switzerland, and the relatively low cost of living in Rome, these years must not have been too taxing in financial terms, though Fuseli was struck down with the fever that was endemic there (turning his hair prematurely – though very romantically – white).

18 *Edgar, Feigning Madness, approaches King Lear* 1772
Pen and wash drawing
61 × 97.5
(24 × 38⅜)
Birmingham
Museums & Art
Gallery

24

The major Shakespearian paintings that Fuseli worked on during his years in Rome have not been identified. However, drawings on Shakespearian subjects from this period are quite numerous, and often on a magnificent scale (fig.18). Notably, the first work he exhibited in London while still in Rome was a drawing, *The Death of Cardinal Beaufort* from Shakespeare's *2 King Henry VI* (fig.19). This is an especially significant work in registering Fuseli's effort to rival and go beyond Hamilton and West in more than just stylistic terms. For a start, the use of Shakespeare as a source was unusual. Though a number of painters had produced important pictures on Shakespearian subjects over the previous decades, notably William Hogarth and Francis Hayman, the potential of the Bard and English literature more generally was only beginning to be explored by British artists. Indeed, contemporaries were concerned that the classical subjects of West and Hamilton were becoming tiresome, and the use of these alternative sources seemed to offer a way forward for British history painting. Still, the composition of Fuseli's drawing bears an obvious resemblance to Hamilton's *Andromache* (fig.9) in its shallow space, lucid arrangement of figures, and the central presence of a dying male figure. The deathbed scene was a particular favourite among later eighteenth-century British history painters, and was a theme frequently shown at the exhibitions and reproduced in prints. While many classical subjects were impenetrable to a wide

19 *The Death of Cardinal Beaufort* 1772
Pen and wash drawing
64.5 × 80
(25⅜ × 31½)
National Museums and Galleries on Merseyside (Walker Art Gallery, Liverpool)

audience, the direct emotional appeal of the deathbed overcame any lack of knowledge on the part of the viewer. Furthermore, by presenting an audience within the picture, some idea of an emotional bond between the pictured onlookers and the actual viewer of the picture could be fabricated, in line with popular ideas about 'sensibility', which stressed the need for such an emotional link with a work of art. Even while mimicking these conventions, Fuseli's drawing revolts against them. Though composed into the general form of a conventional classical deathbed scene, the central, dying figure was definitely not a hero to be admired or sympathised with. Beaufort was a villain, whose depravity was proved when he failed to repent on his deathbed, a scene that was considered as one of the highlights of Shakespeare's works. It is this scene that Fuseli depicts, dramatising the Cardinal's failure to signal his repentance by organising the composition in terms of stark, almost geometric areas of light and shade pointing in towards Beaufort's awkwardly twisted form. If the purpose of history painting was defined as the embodying of noble virtues, particularly the healthy sentimental virtues that appealed to a modern audience, Fuseli's *Beaufort* seems to abandon that aim in favour of sensationalism.

Fuseli's works from the 1770s are unconventional in terms of the technique and process also. Usually, artists of the time would prepare a composition by drawing from life or carefully from antique sculptures, using some kind of soft medium that could trace shifts in tone and texture with great subtlety. A drawing by West of a figure from an antique relief subsequently used as the basis of one of the nude figures in the foreground of the *Pylades and Orestes* is a good example (figs.20, 10). More expressive studies, using pen and ink, would be used to develop the composition as a whole. However, throughout his time in Rome Fuseli only seldom drew directly from life models or the antique, and quite consistently used hard crayons or pen and wash. Only rarely did he attempt to describe gradual tonal changes, preferring to employ dramatic contrasts of tone created by wash or hatching, playing under or against rhythmic patterns of pure contour. This technique, combined with his insistent stylisation of the human form and his frequent use of distorted perspective and scale, mean that his drawings have a highly schematic, abstracted quality, where the design seems to be absolutely determined by the dramatic gestures and looks of his figures, rather than the need to describe pictorial depth or weight. Typically, Fuseli would work on whole compositions, which would be repeated, traced, reversed and rearranged, and then abandoned in an unfinished state (fig.21). Instead of working hard at gradually constructing a composition piece by piece, Fuseli seems always to

20 Benjamin West
Figure from the Orestes Sarcophagus
c.1760–3
Drawing
Swarthmore College, Swarthmore, Pennsylvania

21 *Oedipus Cursing his son Polynices* 1777
Pen and wash drawing
38.9 × 50.2 (15¼ × 19¾)
The National Museum of Fine Arts, Stockholm

be looking for shortcuts: the most abbreviated way of representing a figure, the least time-consuming way of conceiving a dramatic composition. This is an impatient style, rhetorical and declamatory, not diligent and persuasive. It is a style that proclaims sublime genius, rather than proves it. While such idiosyncratic and expressive abstraction would be generally permissible in a preparatory sketch not intended for public display, Fuseli proceeded to translate these qualities very directly into his paintings, maintaining the distortions and simplifications apparent in his drawings through the eschewal of tonal modelling and his use of dramatic contrasts of light and shade. These qualities are evident in his painting of *Oedipus*, one of the finished oils whose design can be dated to his Roman years, which was exhibited at the Academy in 1786 (fig.22).

This playful or experimental approach is most evident in the 'five-point' games Fuseli played with Thomas Banks in Rome. Apparently, the artists would place five dots on a blank sheet of paper, and endeavour to connect those five points by the extremities of a single figure (fig.23). The nature of the exercise meant that the figure was conceived through linear techniques and that it was made to assume extraordinary poses. In itself, the game was not novel: art theorists had advised that it was a most useful practice for an art student to take up in their spare time, encouraging visual ingenuity and facility in the depiction of the body. But with Fuseli the game was not simply an aid to the acquisition of skills as a figurative draughtsman: to judge from the evidence presented – the extraordinary variety of bizarre, illogical poses apparent in his works – it would seem to have contributed to the formulation of finished pictures. The five-point drawing by Fuseli illustrated (fig.23) has been so transformed, by the simple addition of chains and the eagle, into a narrative subject, *Prometheus*. In that respect the practice represents a radical departure from mainstream art theory, which proposed that the artist approached the representation of the ideal through a close attention to nature. In the five-point games, the figure instead emerges out of an arbitrary geometrical scheme. As the famous Italian artist Giambattista Piranesi reportedly exclaimed on seeing one of Fuseli's figure drawings, 'This is not *designing*, but *building* a man.'[11]

Whether derived from a strict adherence to the five-point game or not, Fuseli's graphic work from the Roman years is dominated by seemingly endless reconfigurations of massively muscular bodies whose gestures, by conventional standards, are wholly excessive. Fuseli dismissed the inexpressiveness of contemporary classical art – citing West's *Pylades and Orestes* as a particularly offensive example.[12] West, following Winckelmann's strictures, endeavoured to make his figures conform to the ideal of classical sculpture, in which muscular expression is subsumed to a perfectly smooth whole representative of physical and psychic unity. Fuseli's heavy marking of musculature, derived from mannerist draughtsmanship, could be interpreted as an

22 Oedipus Cursing his son Polynices 1786
Oil on canvas
145 × 165
(57⅛ × 65)
National Gallery of
Art, Washington

23 Prometheus
*c.*1770–1
Pen and wash
drawing
15 × 22.6 (5⅞ × 8⅞)
Öffentliche
Kunstsammlung
Basel,
Kupferstichkabinett

effort to articulate a more fully expressive idea of the body, one which dramatically, even exaggeratedly, communicated narrative, and also registered his presence, as the artist with a very particular approach to draughtsmanship, more fully. Yet, rather like the contemporary body-builders whom Fuseli's figures might remind us of, this also leads to a disintegration of the body into pieces, as each individual muscle becomes swollen and distorted, and the subject of intensive interest even at the expense of the whole.[13] His drawings reduce the human form to a collection of notational marks that are not necessarily immediately descriptive. Rather, any individual mark could represent either the cleavage of a muscle formation, the outline of an individual muscle, or a contour defining the surface of a form, giving his figures an indeterminate status between living flesh, sculpted stone and anatomically excavated corpse (fig.24). In attempting to realise bodies of superhuman power, Fuseli produced a fantasy of the body that was perhaps unsettling and in danger of dissolving. The sheer quantity of his drawings showing ambiguous fragments of bodies, scattered first ideas of impossible forms, or figures cast into irresolvable poses that had to be abandoned, bears witness to that.

Fuseli's drawings and paintings of the 1770s represent two, contradictory, tendencies. On the one hand, there was a concerted effort to go beyond the standards set by Hamilton and West in expression and drama, which served to draw attention to Fuseli's identity as an artist and make him stand out from the crowd. That tendency involved an overblown assertiveness, ensuring that every subject was the most dramatic and violent that could be found, that his draughtsmanship was as expressive and individual as possible, that his heroes were superhuman and gigantic. On the other hand, the process of achieving that aim throws up uncertainties, with regard to the moral content of his subject-matter and the narrative coherence of the bodies he represented.

These issues were recognised by contemporaries, as the newspaper reviews

29

24 *Roman Scene*
*c.*1771
Pen and wash
drawing
36.7 × 47.6
(14½ × 18¾)
The British Museum

of an important, lost picture he sent back to the Royal Academy exhibition in London in 1777 made evident. The catalogue recorded Fuseli's painting simply as 'No.127. A Scene from Macbeth', and it has been identified with a rather small painting of *Macbeth and the Armed Head*. However, critics of the time noted the larger than life scale of the picture.[14] The *Morning Chronicle* also refers to the large size of the figures as well as hinting at the picture's composition and subject matter:

> Mr Fusole's scene of Macbeth shows a fine poetical imagination,
> although the enormous size of the figures and the disposition of the
> Witches over Macbeth's head, rather serve to prove that such a scene
> never existed in nature than to give coinage to the brain currency. The
> vision of the Ghosts of Kings *that shall be*, is finely conceived and
> expressed.
>
> (*Morning Chronicle*, 28 April 1777)

On the basis of these descriptions, the exhibited painting can be identified as a painted version of the large drawing of *The Witches Show Macbeth Banquo's Descendants* (fig.25). Although reviewers were generally favourable to the picture, there were concerns that in exercising his imagination too freely Fuseli had exceeded the bounds of good taste. The material appearance of the picture was criticised, with one reviewer quipping 'it may be said there is too much Poetry, and not enough painting in this Piece' (*St James's Chronicle*, 24–6 April 1777). Another commentator, in the *General Advertiser*, is particularly telling:

> of all the scenes yet taken from our immortal Poet, perhaps this is the
> most extravagant. – The portrait of Macbeth is infinitely larger than

the life & from the attitude puts one in mind of a gigantic Quixot fighting the windmills – In short it plainly appears, the painter aimed at something great, & we must confess he has succeeded – in point of size.[15]

Fuseli's ambition is here comically deflated. His superhuman Macbeth is compared to the elderly non-hero Don Quixote in Cervantes's famous and popular comic novel (first published 1605–18). His imagination fuelled by romantic fiction, Don Quixote imagined himself a great knight, fighting heroically and nobly, but in reality only chasing windmills and appearing a senile old fool. Fuseli's overblown hero, and his own ambitions as an artist, could be seen as having such qualities, offering up a timeless vision of superheroic strength and ghostly spectres in an age of self-conscious reason, science and fashionable fripperies. If this picture can properly be considered a summation of all Fuseli's ambitions in the 1770s, the writer in the *General Advertiser* might be considered as his most acute critic.

25 *The Witches Show Macbeth Banquo's Descendants* 1773–9
Pen and wash drawing
36 × 42
(14⅛ × 16½)
Kunsthaus Zurich

2

'SHOCKINGLY MAD,
MADDER THAN EVER'

Fuseli finally set out from Rome in the autumn of 1778. The wars between America and Britain had escalated into a European conflict, stymieing the Grand Tour, and having the knock-on effect of sending living costs in Italy soaring. After over eight years in the cultural capital of Europe, Fuseli was obliged to relaunch himself as an artist in London. Something of his self-proclaimed ambition at that moment is signalled in a caricature drawing sent to the younger English painter James Northcote on his journey through northern Italy (fig.26). A gigantic male figure recalling both Fuseli's heroically conceived figures (figs.11, 25) and Sergel's caricature of the artist (fig.17) is shown straddling a schematic map of Europe. To the top left, a set of male genitals with wings flies towards Italy – a bawdy expression of the artist's greatest hopes and desires. At the bottom of the image is 'England', occupied by two thin mice identified as Fuseli's friends, the artists Ozias Humphrey and George Romney, and a third, fat rodent, named as George III's favourite history painter, Benjamin West. In the accompanying letter, Fuseli warned Northcote to 'Take heed of the mice'.[1] They present a moral about the chasm that had opened up between the majority of artists and the favoured few. Fuseli was well aware that pursuing a career as an artist in Britain would be arduous, though potentially rewarding. His views on his native Switzerland should be self-explanatory.

Fuseli's years in Rome saw him taking less interest than ever in German-speaking culture. His correspondence with his old Swiss friends began to dwindle, and news of new German literature was greeted with indifference. Yet the journey back to England provided the opportunity for what was to be his last visit to Switzerland itself. This led to a couple of complicated romantic entanglements, resulting in some characteristically stormy and overheated poetic musings on his part. He also received some artistic commissions. The most notable of these was the large *Oath of the Ruttli*, destined for Zurich town hall and commemorating the medieval confederacy that established Zurich as a republic (fig.27). This work shows the dynamic and virile conception of the male body Fuseli had developed on the model of Michelangelo and sixteenth-century mannerist art being applied, with great pictorial economy, to a serious subject from history, giving the rather abstract theme of political action a purely physical expression. A similar strategy is apparent even in the unpromising subject of his self-portrait with the elderly Bodmer painted at the same time and exhibited in London in 1781 (fig.28). With the sitters depicted as two intellectuals, disposed in doubtless very highbrow conversation either

26 *Caricature of the
Artist Leaving Italy*
1778
Ink drawing
24.5 × 19.3
(9⅝ × 7⅝)
Kunsthaus Zurich

side of a bust of Homer, the picture nonetheless conveys a quite alarming sense of physical energy, right down to the sinewy fingers of the painter pressed in meditation on his temple. Like the gigantic figure in his caricature of 1778, Fuseli wanted to show himself always taking heroic strides, even if he was only painting a couple of Swiss men of letters in their study.

The London art world that Fuseli returned to early in 1779 was of a markedly different character from the one he left nine years earlier. In 1770 there was a tremendous sense of optimism about British artistic culture. In the intervening decade, the very success of the Academy in encouraging artists' aspirations had created problems. The market simply did not expand to support them, and in particular, Reynolds's professed aim to 'make Historical Painters' of his students failed to find material support.[2] The King's commissions for subject pictures were virtually monopolised by West, while two major schemes for historical painting intended to set a precedent for public patronage, the decoration of St Paul's Cathedral and of the Great Room of the Society of Arts in London, fizzled out. In a letter written in the spring of 1774, barely half a decade since the creation of the Academy, its treasurer, Sir William Chambers, wrote in a private letter of the plight of the younger generation of artists: 'at present they have little or no encouragement, we are over-stocked with Artists of all Sorts, and it will soon be as necessary to have an Hospital for the Support of decayed Vertuosi [i.e. artists] as it was a few years ago to establish an Academy to raise them'.[3]

Worse still was to come during the period of the wars with America (1776–82), which many believed had a direct and damaging impact on art

27 *The Oath of the*
Ruttli 1779–81
Oil on canvas
267 × 178
(105 × 70⅛)
Kunsthaus Zurich

patronage. Yet in 1780 the Academy defiantly moved to new, purpose-built rooms in Somerset House, the most ambitious public building of eighteenth-century London. With that relocation, it secured a permanent place in the heart of the capital and public consciousness, at the expense of the competing exhibiting groups who declined and eventually disappeared. The annual exhibition of modern British art became an established part of the social season. As early illustrations of the exhibition hall filled with a cross-section of fashionable London society show, it was a place to see art, but also to be seen (fig.29). For some critics, it was not only the visitors who were encouraged to show off at the exhibitions. The artists themselves, forced to compete for attention in an exhibition always crammed with pictures, were beginning to make art specifically to grab the limelight. A letter of 1782 provides a vivid characterisation of the exhibition as the site of fashionable display for artists *and* visitors:

> there is a fashionable Rage which seems to prevail here for some late years, which is gratified at the moderate Expence of a Shilling a Visit. I mean the different Exhibitions of the Works of English Artists ... To these Places of Publick Resort, do People Flock in a forenoon to

28 *The Painter in*
Conversation with
Johann Jakob Bodmer
1778–81
Oil on canvas
163 × 150
(64⅛ × 59)
Kunsthaus Zurich

saunter about gazing at each other as at any other kind of Route [social gathering], and now and then perhaps look with admiration on an *Outré* Piece, that on account of its staring Colours and sharp unnatural Angles would *attrappe* their Notice.[4]

This suggests reciprocity between the 'gazing' crowd and the 'staring' pictures, and the use of French terms conjures up a sense of fashionable affectation. With this in mind, we can consider the exhibitions as a decisive factor in the way art developed in the later eighteenth century. Artists tried various ways of getting the notice of the general public – from the modern-life history paintings by West and others that represented events currently in the news, to the grand portraits of famous actresses and military heroes by Reynolds and Thomas Gainsborough that fed into and reacted to gossip and propaganda. The letters and diaries of artists record the importance attached to getting pictures in the public eye by showing them in a good position in the exhibition. Critics and commentators often expressed anxiety about this competition for audience attention. In particular, criticisms emerged of the 'singularity' of works on bizarre and supernatural subjects that were getting a lot of press. In 1783 Horace Walpole complained of the way modern artists 'have attempted to paint Deities, Visions, Witchcraft &c, but have only been bombast & extravagant, without true dignity'.[5] Two years later a newspaper critic similarly noted that 'Gypsies, witches, and flying Devils seem to have engrossed the attention of many artists' (*Universal Daily Register*, 2 May 1785). In the absence of any effective policy for encouraging historical art, novel forms of painting developed that mimicked many of the conventions of high art, traditionally defined, but emphasising the peculiarities of the artist and encompassing sensationalist subject-matter calculated to appeal to the lowest common denominator. At the head of this phenomenon was the acknowledged master of surprise and singularity, Henry Fuseli.

The works that Fuseli exhibited in the 1780s added up to a concerted effort to make such a name for himself, in direct competition with his contemporaries. In the summer of 1780 Fuseli visited Sir Joshua Reynolds's studio and saw him at work on a canvas depicting a tragic subject from Virgil's *Aeneid*, *The*

29 Pietro Martini
after J.H. Ramberg
The Exhibition at the Royal Academy at Somerset House 1787
1787
Engraving
Royal Academy of Arts, London

Death of Dido (fig. 30). Reynolds was the most famous artist in Britain, and the leading proponent of the 'Great Style'. Although much more occupied with portraits, in painting *The Death of Dido* Reynolds was setting out to epitomise what the Great Style was meant to be, with its serious theme from classical literature and 'old-masterly' look. Yet Fuseli saw that he was faltering, noting that Reynolds 'himself begins to think he has failed'.[6] He immediately set about executing his own version of precisely the same subject for Sir Robert Smyth, a patron he had met in Italy (fig. 31), with a view to issuing a challenge to the President's authority as a history painter and hoping to accrue by association some of the extensive press coverage that always accompanied Reynolds's exhibited works. It appears that the strategy succeeded, in that when both pictures were exhibited, facing each other, at the Royal Academy in 1781, Fuseli received an unprecedented number of press notices, several of which compared his work directly with Reynolds's.[7] He seems very deliberately to have produced a painting that would contrast with Reynolds's version of the subject. Where the president employed, quite reasonably (if also predictably), a horizontal canvas to accommodate the supine figure of Dido, Fuseli produced a more complex composition on an inconveniently vertical format that rested for its effect upon dramatic (and technically difficult) foreshortening. Where Reynolds has concentrated upon the evocation of texture and depth through the loading and manipulation of the painted surface, evoking Baroque precedents, Fuseli reduces his figures to volumes whose surfaces are relatively plain, and certainly are not modulated texturally. And where the President uses melding tones and heavy drapery to give a sense of substance and weight, Fuseli's painting is much more concerned with creating a complicated, linear design characterised by sharp contrasts of form and tone.

30 Joshua Reynolds
The Death of Dido
1781
Oil on canvas
147.3 × 239.4
(58 × 94¼)
The Royal Collection

31 *The Death of Dido*
1781
Oil on canvas
243 × 183
(95⅔ × 72)
Yale Center for
British Art, Paul
Mellon Collection

We may have some doubts about how well Fuseli has achieved his aims in this work. However, if the trickiness of this image was intended to announce his artistic aspirations and individuality, he certainly succeeded. The review by 'A Friend to the Arts' in the *St James's Chronicle* (28 April–1 May 1781) was especially revealing:

> Something might be said on the Manner in which the Figures are placed in the Picture; one above the other, which is not allowed to be a good Composition. We must attribute it to a Kind of Singularity aimed at by the Artist. Criticks should not be too severe on that Head; first, because it is often productive of excellent Effects; and secondly, if we do not allow Artists to be singular, they will be apt to fall into a disgustful Sameness. The Italian Schools are famous above all others, on Account of the great Variety of Stile they afford. As soon as Painters began to imitate each other, they were undone. The French School was ruined by that alone, from the very first Period of its Excellence.

Singularity, even when it was at the expense of the established rules, or even quality, was emerging as a defining feature of the national culture, according to a range of commentators. Shakespeare, for instance, was reckoned great because of his flouting of the rules of literary composition, which was never permitted in the classical theatre of France. Here, the idea of singularity is brought into play to validate Fuseli's flawed attempt at greatness.

According to this critic, even if the artist has failed, he at least tried to be himself, and that makes him better than the artists on the Continent. If nothing else, this was a fine alibi for Fuseli's more basic desire to distinguish himself in the context of the exhibition, and gain public notice and, it was hoped, extra business.

Despite the heightened public awareness of Fuseli's work at the beginning of the 1780s, commissions were still scarce. Among the most substantial from this period was the subject taken from Dryden's *Theodore and Honoria*, painted for the Earl of Orford (fig. 32). The commission originated when the Italian decorative painter G.B. Cipriani, who was originally engaged to paint four pictures 'with subjects out of Homer and Dryden's fables' for the Earl, died before the series was complete.[8] The paintings executed by Cipriani were conventional works of the Anglo-Italian classical revival, employing a stagelike setting, clear gestures and expressions, and 'archaeological' details (fig. 33). While Fuseli's picture was on the same format as Cipriani's, as in the case of *Dido* he produced a work that contrasted starkly with that of his senior contemporary. It employs dramatic chiaroscuro, a dynamic and centrifugal composition, and includes characteristically elongated figures disposed in a

32 *Theodore Meets in the Wood the Spectre of His Ancestor Guido Cavalcanti c.*1783
Oil on canvas
276 × 317
(108 × 124¾)
The National Museum of Western Art, Tokyo

33 Giovanni Battista
Cipriani
*Philoctetes on the
Island of Lemnos* 1781
Oil on canvas
275.5 × 319.4
(108½ × 125¾)
Spencer House

manner that suggests extreme physical exertion. As in the *Dido*, the treatment of anatomy is highly stylised: the figure of the woman is characterised by sharply intersecting, almost abstract volumes and her head is twisted back in a wholly unnatural fashion; Theodore is shown in a skin-tight costume, the cleavage of his muscles deeply scored. Where the Italian artist presents a scene with the compositional and spatial stability directly evocative of seventeenth-century classical art and, of course, the classical art of the 1760s, Fuseli's references are to the violent contortions of mannerist art, and he employs a low viewpoint to disconcerting effect.

Such an ambitious commission, from a member of the aristocracy, the traditional source of art patronage, was to remain a rarity throughout Fuseli's career, as it was for almost all his contemporaries in the field of history painting. Although he did receive commissions 'face to face', notably from a small circle of self-consciously intellectual provincial professionals, and later the Lock family of Norbury and the Countess of Guilford, far more innovative and significant was Fuseli's manipulation of the anonymous art public. Through the 1780s Fuseli painted a series of pictures that were very clearly meant as a means of getting public attention. Drawn from classical or English literature, these concentrate on scenes of spectacle, drama, eroticism and the supernatural (fig.34). These were images calculated to catch the eye of the exhibition visitor, even when painted on quite a small scale. While Fuseli sold few of the paintings, he was able to derive material profit through the publication of prints. In the 1780s Fuseli issued eight high-quality mezzotints relating to exhibited works, working closely with the print publisher and engraver John

Raphael Smith, who was then trying to establish himself in the field (fig. 35). Rather than simply documenting Fuseli's works, these were independent commodities intended to make a profit, and, though not cheap, were available to a much larger market than were unique paintings. Given the eminent suitability of Fuseli's paintings from this period to reproduction in the medium of mezzotint – a form of engraving that represents its subject through tone rather than line – we might even speculate whether he was developing paintings characterised by stark contrasts of tone with an eye to this larger market.

The self-consciousness of Fuseli's manipulation of public interest in his works is demonstrated most vividly in the sequence of imaginary subjects that he exhibited and published in this period. Conventionally, history paintings were always based on an existing literary or historical source. Writers on art had put great store by the painter's ability effectively to depict an incident or theme represented in textual form. In particular, traditional art theory had promoted the idea that an effective work of art would represent, as Fuseli himself put it, 'The middle moment, the moment of suspense, the crisis ... big with the past and pregnant with the future'.[9] This depended, of course, on the viewer being able to identify the literary source – and artists often introduced references or even whole quotes into their entries in exhibition catalogues to facilitate this. Fuseli played on this by painting themes that the broad mass of the literate public who attended exhibitions would be familiar with – Shakespeare, Milton and classical literature. Yet he also exhibited paintings on themes drawn from the obscure legends of Northern Europe that were only

34 *The Three Witches*
1783
Oil on canvas
65 × 91.5 (25⅝ × 36)
Kunsthaus Zurich

35 John Raphael
Smith after Henry
Fuseli
*Lady Macbeth
Walking in her Sleep*
1784
Mezzotint
62.5 × 45.2
(24⅜ × 17¾)
Kunsthaus Zurich

beginning to gain an audience. Most startlingly of all, in the early 1780s he also painted and exhibited scenes that had no specific literary sources, starting with the *Ezzelin and Meduna* of 1780 (fig.36). The full title given in the exhibition catalogue was 'Ezzelin Musing over the Body of his Wife Meduna, Slain by him for her Infidelity During his Absence on the Crusades', which provides more than enough information for the viewer to elaborate a whole narrative around this scene. In fact, there is no literary source for this scene – as Lord Byron must have found many years later, when the poet sought fruitlessly for the subject in Italian literature.[10] The painter had invented the story himself, even preparing a sketch of an alternative incident in this projected narrative a few years earlier. Similarly, the *Percival Delivering Belisane from the Enchantment of Urma* shown in 1783 has no specific literary source, though the exhibition catalogue claimed it was drawn from the tales of Thyot, itself the fictional source of Wolfram von Eschenbach's *Parzival* (1477) (fig.37). We might also count the original, exhibited version of the famous *Nightmare* in this class, as its subject derives from no specific text (fig.1).

In a letter to his patron William Roscoe of Liverpool written in 1791, Fuseli explains something of his intentions in painting such pictures. At that time the painter was endeavouring to progress with a series of monumental canvases based on Milton, which he refers to: 'Your approbation of my proposal for painting Small pictures to make the Large ones [i.e. his Milton series] go on, gives me much pleasure ... Such Situations as I have Combined Such as Ezelin, Belisane &c; Philosophical Ideas made intuitive, or Sentiment personified, suit, in my opinion, Small Canvases eminently.'[11] Here Fuseli refers to his invented scenes as particularly marketable commodities. The works he executed for Roscoe, and for the circle of provincial businessmen and professionals Roscoe introduced him to, were on the whole on a relatively small scale. And of the eight mezzotints he issued in the 1780s, three were related to his 'Combined' images – the *Ezzelin and Meduna*, the *Nightmare*, and a separate scene from the story of *Percival and Belisane* (a story which, however, never existed) (fig.38). Given that Fuseli exhibited eighteen canvases in this period, mainly on Shakespearian, Miltonic and classical themes, this is significantly out of proportion. These images show the way that, faced with a socially mixed audience in the exhibition hall, in direct competition with other works of art, the role of a painting was not necessarily to fulfil the traditional demands of art as a form of illustration of noble themes. It could embody a much more vaguely conceived idea and serve as a spectacle in its own right, simply to stir interest.

Although none of his viewers or critics could really have known the story being depicted, these images are laden with clues. Besides the descriptive titles given in the exhibition catalogues and on the prints, the costumes and settings conjure up a world that was increasingly familiar to a broad audience – the world of Gothic literature. This was a new genre of popular writing, dealing

36 *Ezzelin and Meduna* 1779
Oil on canvas
45.7 × 50.8
(18 × 20)
Sir John Soane's Museum

with tales of ghosts and witches, revenge and heroism, and bitter sexual intrigues in fantastical medieval settings. Really an early form of pulp fiction, it was deliberately populist, and discarded many of the narrative and descriptive conventions of traditional writing in favour of sensationalism.[12] Its use of medieval settings, fantasy and terror was directed at the lowest common denominator, while being legitimated as expressions of the sublime, the aesthetic category concerned with the power of shock and horror. The heroes and heroines of Gothic literature are merely ciphers, acting out dramas with no commonly understood moral content or direction, but merely acting for the sake of sensationalism. With its mysterious, shallow characters and jumbled narrative, the Gothic represents a world defined through transitory instances of personal interaction and exchange, moments of irrational drama, rather than the fixed certainties that come with a logical, developed linear narrative. In that sense, it represents by its very form the sensationalism and uncertainty that characterised the emerging consumerist society – a society founded on ephemeral consumer choices and rapidly shifting schemes of social fashion and distinction that displaced the fixed social hierarchies that were imagined to exist before. Fuseli's paintings of the early 1780s deserve to be interpreted as painterly examples of this Gothic sublime not only because they share many of the trappings of its literary cousin, but because they

37 Percival Delivering Belisane from the Enchantment of Urma
1783
Oil on canvas
99 × 125 (39 × 49¼)
Tate

38 John Raphael
Smith after Henry
Fuseli
*Belisane and
Percival under the
Enchantment of Urma*
1782
Mezzotint
43.5 × 55.1
(17⅛ × 21⅝)
The British Museum

BELISANE & PARCIVAL *under the* ENCHANTMENT *of* URMA

similarly straddle the division between high culture, with its sublime ambitions, and popular culture. His heroes and heroines are similarly shallow, and they do not have relationships we can know about other than those revealed pictorially by the artist. In the spaces of the exhibition, the image could serve as, primarily, an instant spectacle without necessarily embodying the heroic and ethical paradigms traditionally considered as the main aim of high art intended for a socially exclusive audience. As with the Gothic novel, Fuseli's exhibition pictures were products of the commercialisation of culture that also commented on the effects of consumerism on personal identity.

The Gothic sublime apparent in popular literature and in Fuseli's paintings also has a nostalgic aspect. In eschewing moral and narrative certainties, a different kind of certainty is projected onto the very bodies of their fantasy characters. The protagonists of the Gothic act out stereotypical roles recalling (like Don Quixote) a lost world of chivalry and heroism in which men were men and women were women. Hence the often stark gendering of visual form in Fuseli's imagery, where all the heroes are supermen, with elongated limbs, pronounced muscles, armour and absurdly phallic weaponry, and all the young women are fleshy and curvaceous, caricatured signs of passive or depraved femininity. The figures in the *Perceval*, the beautiful maiden and the muscular hero, are ciphers expressing a highly stylised differentiation of sexual identity. In this, his paintings can be interpreted as, like the Gothic novel, a response to the developing uncertainties around gender, apparent in contemporary criticism of the narcissistic, feminising effects of consumerism and the emergence of early feminist literature. Such a schematic distinction between the sexes was also a feature of his old friend Lavater's popular

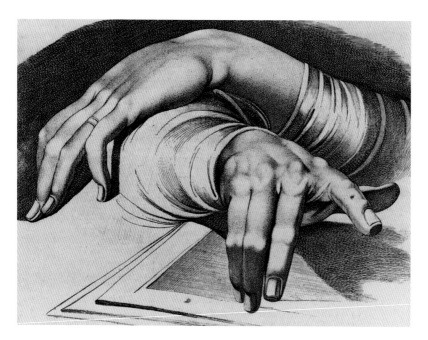

39 Johann Heinrich
Lips after Henry
Fuseli
*Man and Woman's
Crossed Hands*
Engraving from
Johann Casper
Lavater, *Essai sur la
Physiognomie* (La
Haye, 1781–6)
17 × 22 (6¾ × 8⅝)
The British Library
[29.g.7]

writings on physiognomy (the quasi-science of deducing the moral and intellectual qualities of a person on the basis of their physical appearance). Like
physiognomic theory, Fuseli's pictures seemed to offer simple, visible signs for
reading sexual status in an era of shifting identities. Fuseli himself provided
a series of illustrations for the original German and French editions of his
Physiognomical Fragments, and assisted in the English translation, published in
three volumes by Joseph Johnson in 1789–98. One of his designs shows a pair
of hands that can be interpreted as a distillation of Fuseli's approach to the
human figure; the male hand is active, dramatically foreshortened, the
woman's lifeless, flat, lacking muscular definition (fig.39). Seen as a synec-
doche (a device by which the whole is represented by a part), this pair of hands
could stand in for Ezzelin and Meduna, or Perceval and Belisane, or virtually
any of Fuseli's heroes and heroines.

If Fuseli's paintings of the 1780s can rightly be read as frank attempts
to court public interest, the press criticism of his day would seem to testify to
his success. The artist was the subject of extensive commentary with every
exhibit. What is particularly evident in this criticism is a sense of ambivalence.
As a critic commented, he was seen as 'the worst as well as the best of painters
in the room' (*Public Advertiser*, 4 May 1786). For his supporters, Fuseli was the
imaginative genius bar none; he may have lacked technical skills, he may have
produced subjects that were bizarre or obscure, but these were but aspects,
indeed indications, of the extent of his genius. His critics, on the other hand,
were often just baffled:

> It is a difficult task to estimate the merits of this artist's work, by any
> rule or criterion by which we judge of others. Pictures are, or ought to
> be, a representation of natural objects, delineated with taste and

precision. Mr *Fuseli* gives us the human figure, from the recollection of its form, and not from the form itself; he seems to be painting every thing from fancy, which renders his work almost incomprehensible, and leaves no criterion to judge of them by, but the imagination.

(*Public Advertiser*, 22 May 1786)

Sometimes this provided the opportunity for the critic to claim that his works were in a 'superior' taste that required a particularly refined mind (like that of the critic, presumably) to interpret. Sometimes, at the opposite extreme, this 'fancy' was imagined as having a psychiatric origin. Fuseli might be admired for 'the enthusiasm and eccentricity' of his imagination, but he was also attacked for letting his 'genius run mad' (*Morning Post*, 5 May 1785). Standing before one of Fuseli's witchcraft scenes at the exhibition of 1785, Horace Walpole only noted in the margins of his catalogue: 'shockingly mad, madder than ever; quite mad' (fig.40).[13] There were stories of his eating pork to conjure nightmare scenes in his sleep, or taking opium (which he admitted he did, but only for medicinal purposes), or, quite simply, being a lunatic.[14]

Fuseli and his art occupied a knife-edge between the sublime and the ridiculous, twisting or disregarding convention in a potentially insane effort to achieve effects of grandeur. This was never more evident than in the

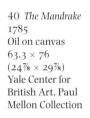

40 *The Mandrake*
1785
Oil on canvas
63.3 × 76
(24⅞ × 29⅞)
Yale Center for
British Art, Paul
Mellon Collection

assessments of his treatment of the human form: 'Fuseli would have some pretensions to a twig of the historical laurel, if he could ever paint a figure without breaking its limbs' (*Morning Post*, 6 June 1788). Or, in a disturbing analogy: 'Mr Fuseli would have made an excellent *Poulterer*, he has such a happy knack of twisting legs and arms, without any regard to fractures or dislocations.'[15] The violence of the language in such reports registers the doubts about his work, an anxiety vividly summed up in a letter written in 1789 by the Devonshire watchmaker Samuel Northcote to his brother, the painter James, in London: 'some of the first things which I saw of his, and which happened to sute his manner I thought very good but now his things disgust one as Bread and Flesh may when helped out with a Fishey Knife'.[16] In the idealised language of art theory, 'taste' was a purely intellectual faculty. Although it was acknowledged that aesthetic taste originated in the basic bodily senses, it was claimed that modern (white, socially elite) men were possessed of a pure, transcendental notion of taste that referred to the realm of art and culture, rather than the democratic senses of the body.[17] What Samuel Northcote suggests is that Fuseli's work forces the viewer to revert to the older, bodily definition. His paintings might function not so much as 'art', but more simply as objects of guttural disgust, demolishing any opportunity for the social pretension that the exercise of taste was meant to provide.

During the 1780s Fuseli effectively turned himself into a brand through the exhibitions. He developed a style that was instantly recognisable and always commented on. The controversy around his art established him as a public figure, when being a public figure meant selling more prints and maybe attracting commissions. Moreover, it meant that the lack of certainty that surrounded the role of art in modern, consumer society, was exploited to his advantage. If Fuseli was said to be eccentric or insane, the oddness of his paintings could (reassuringly) be explained with reference to his personality rather than any of the larger structures of the art world. But if his genius operated so far beyond normal convention that it might be cast as the result of mental illness, what would that mean for any artist who might imitate him? The need to establish a distinctive British School of history painting was a major topic of discussion; the Academy had been founded with exactly that intention. Fuseli's association with madness and eccentricity meant that he could hardly be imagined helping to build this School in any normal way. His 'madness' could, though, be conveyed by some other means:

> When the Second George proposed General Wolfe to command the expedition to Quebec, the Duke of Newcastle begged his Majesty to consider that the man was mad; 'if he is mad' replied the old Monarch, 'if he is mad, I wish to God he would bite some of my Generals'. In like manner we have often wished that Mr Fuseli would bite some of our cold-blooded artists of the present day. They would then be marked by something.
>
> (*The Diary*, 26 May 1789)

The artist who was most readily compared to Fuseli in the 1780s was Maria Cosway. During that decade she exhibited a series of paintings on obscure literary themes, emphasising the supernatural and horrific aspects of the subject (fig.41). In their dramatic lighting effects, supernatural elements and idiosyncratic handling of the human form these pictures owe a great deal to Fuseli's example. It was reckoned that 'Her stile is nearer that of *Fuseli* than any other modern artist.'[18] But it was not imagined that she was simply influenced by Fuseli. Rather, she had been infected. As a critic noted in response to Cosway's pictures in 1785, 'Heaven help us, she has caught the *Fuzeli*' (*Morning Chronicle*, 18 May 1785). Constantly re-created as an artist and a man through unregulated art criticism, gossip and anecdote, Fuseli became less of an artist in the conventional sense, who teaches and influences others within the institutionalised setting of the studio or school, and rather more like a cultural virus.

CREUSA APPEARING TO ÆNEAS.

41 Valentine Green after Maria Cosway *Creusa Appearing to Aeneas* 1781 Mezzotint The British Museum

3

'HUMOUR, PATHOS, TERROR, BLOOD'

The first two decades of Fuseli's career as a full-time artist in Rome and London saw the formation of a highly personal style and a distinctive range of subject-matter, and the effective, though largely improvised, marketing of these to a small clique of patrons and friends and to an art public in the process of defining itself. Through this period, Fuseli's career can be understood in terms of his own career motivations coinciding with the growth of new markets for art and novel kinds of publicity. At the end of the 1780s his singularity was cast into different, more formalised frameworks. In 1788 he was elected an Associate Member of the Royal Academy, followed in 1790 by election as a full member. Fuseli, widely considered the most eccentric artist of his generation, became a fully paid-up member of the art establishment. Over the same period, he was involved in a series of successful commercial art galleries. In 1786 John Boydell announced plans for his Shakespeare Gallery, signalling a new kind of art venture. Fuseli produced a series of canvases for Boydell, and for the other entrepreneurial schemes that followed, and ultimately opened his own, and in the event spectacularly *uncommercial* gallery, the Milton Gallery. Relevant to understanding both Fuseli's role in the Academy and the new galleries is the emergence of an idea of the British School of painting more articulate and persuasive than before, and intimately connected to the rising nationalism of this period – the years of Britain's long and fraught wars against revolutionary France.

Fuseli's election as a full member of the Royal Academy provided the occasion for the production of a painting that can be interpreted as the clearest statement of the artistic ideals represented by his work– *Thor Battering the Midgard Serpent* (fig.42). As such, it is worth considering at some length. The Academy demanded that every newly elected member would hand over a painting or sculpture, for which he would receive the official diploma naming him as an Academician. This, the Diploma Work, was meant to be a typical example of his art, and would contribute to the formation of a gallery of exemplary works of British art. While the Academy was set up to create a school of history painters, in fact most of its members worked in the 'lesser' genres of portraiture, landscape and 'fancy pictures', and the pictures submitted as Diploma Works generally reflect this. Fuseli, however, was an exception, and the work he presented makes great efforts to draw attention to the fact.

In terms of its subject-matter alone, Fuseli's Diploma Work makes a point of the singularity of its painter. The subject is drawn from the ancient Ice-

42 *Thor Battering the Midgard Serpent* 1790
Oil on canvas
131 × 91
(51⅝ × 35⅞)
Royal Academy of Arts, London

landic epic, *The Edda*, and concerns the hero Thor's revenge upon the monstrous Midgard Serpent. Fuseli shows Thor in the boat of the giant Eymer, raising his club to strike the serpent while the god Odin looks on from the clouds. The source of Fuseli's picture could be described as recondite, in that *The Edda*, and Scandinavian literature as a whole, was very rarely translated, quite neglected by scholars, and stood outside the traditions of classical literature that were the most prized. Instead, it is drawn from the less established world of popular literature. The English translation of *The Edda* in David Mallet's *Northern Antiquities* (1770) had been quite a success, suiting the taste for Gothic fantasy and legend, where exactly this sort of 'obscurity' conveyed a valuable mystique. So, the picture both testified to the surprising and idiosyncratic character of Fuseli as an artist and maintained the superficial gloss of intellectual exclusivity that was occasionally attached to his work.

The picture expresses Fuseli's singularity most visibly in the treatment of the figure of Thor. The nude or barely-draped male figure was an emblem of artistic expertise. Life drawing was the foundation stone of Academic art practice, and in theory every artist of ambition should aspire to the painting of heroically conceived male bodies, in the tradition of the greatest ancient and Renaissance artists. Great importance was attached to the correct drawing of the human form, especially the ability to make the articulation of the various parts of the body convincing in every detail. By those standards, Fuseli's conception of his hero's body is faulty. At a number of points, his drawing falters or is quite deliberately fudged. Thor's right arm is covered by his cloak, so the tricky foreshortening it would have needed is avoided, the legs intersect awkwardly and unconvincingly with the torso, and the left foot is hidden from view, leaving a row of schematic toes propped up on the side of the boat without visible support. Fuseli had produced a figure that demanded to be understood in terms of the artist's 'singularity' and 'genius', rather than the established conventions of picture-making.

Despite these very apparent faults, the figure of Thor none the less communicates a sense of vaulting ambition in its reference to other art. The dramatic play of light and shade over his form and the pallor given to his skin invoke the model of ancient marble sculpture. The figure's heroic pose and proportions recall Renaissance and baroque paintings of St Michael and, especially, Michelangelo's figure of Christ in the *Last Judgement*. By making these transparent references to heroic art, Fuseli is proclaiming his 'genius'. He is also attempting to restate a supposedly timeless ideal of the perfected male physique. The hugely muscular body of Thor can be read as an effort to make a statement about the manly hero, in an age of anxiety about manliness itself. The widening availability of luxury goods unsettled traditional assumptions about the class system, and about the different nature of men and women. There were great concerns that men were becoming more occupied with fripperies and fashion, usually identified as 'feminine', while women were able to assert greater control over their lives and the society around them through their participation in the new commercial spaces of public entertainment and social activity. Fuseli himself was frequently vehement in his condemnation of the confusion about sex roles: 'In an age of luxury women have taste, decide and dictate; for in an age of luxury woman aspires to the function of man, and man slides into the offices of woman. The epoch of eunuchs was ever the epoch of viragos.'[1] The revolutionary political events of the era – from the America uprising of 1776 through to the French Revolution (contemporaneous with the production of the *Thor*) – made the potential for change all the more evident. These revolutions encompassed a rethinking of the relative roles of men and women in society, evident most famously in the feminist writings of Mary Wollstonecraft, whom Fuseli knew at this time. Their relationship made him all too aware that he was living in an 'epoch of viragos'. She became enamoured of the now middle-aged but recently married Fuseli, and pursued him so relentlessly that Mrs Fuseli banned her from their house. It may have been Wollstonecraft that Fuseli was thinking of when he later said, '*I hate clever women*; they are only troublesome.'[2]

Yet if the body of Thor is meant as an unequivocal statement of a fully masculine form, we might argue Fuseli's picture is not entirely frank or straightforward. Thor's facial features, for instance, correspond to the feminine type found in the 'rococo' paintings of François Boucher and his followers, and the light and shade that describe the chest is so emphatic that there is the suggestion of breasts (a familiar enough trait in musclemen of our own day, from Victor Mature to Arnold Schwarzenegger). Furthermore, Thor's genitals are hidden by shade (though the wedge of light on the underside of the left thigh can be read as a displaced, and quite chunky, male member). Fuseli's great efforts to create a body that is absolutely muscular, massive and manly has resulted in a figure with distinctly female characteristics. These aspects of the painting acknowledge the potential of the male nude to become an object of desire (like, in the dominant view of the time, a woman). Contemporaries were

43 *A Woman Before the Laocoön* 1801–5
Pen and pencil drawing
32 × 40.4
(12⅝ × 15⅞)
Kunsthaus Zurich

acutely aware that in the current day, the enjoyment of the male nude was not always securely aesthetic and transcendental. In the ideal situation projected by high-minded art theorists, the art nude was something looked at in a highly controlled setting in exclusive (and exclusively male) aristocratic company. In reality, the heroic male form was in one way or another available to all-comers for the price of a ticket to the exhibition or in mass-produced form in prints or sculptural reproductions in an increasingly wide range of public and private spaces. In these contexts, even young women might be exposed to the most explicit images – a point Fuseli himself commented on in an amusing drawing of a well-dressed young woman literally taken aback at the sight of the ancient *Laocoön* (fig.43). The point to be made is that in Fuseli's time even the noblest conceptions of the male body were potentially subject to erotically charged ways of looking. Where these encounters were commented on – in the literature of the Grand Tour, or in Thomas Rowlandson's comic images on the theme – this way of looking would generally be projected onto an imagined female or emasculated viewer. This would seem to be a role played within Fuseli's image by the comic figures of the cowardly giant Eymer and the miniature, elderly Odin. They are cast as voyeurs whose gazes both channel and try to mitigate the potentially desiring, erotic look of the actual viewer.[3] It may even be taken that Thor's own girlish features establish a narcissistic gaze that makes the viewer more self-conscious about enjoying the appearance of his body.

In interpreting *Thor Battering the Midgard Serpent* as a fraught attempt to establish an idea of a fully masculine hero, the way it is painted is especially significant. Thor's body is described in a very restrained way, in that the paint is laid on thinly and evenly. Together with the almost monochrome colour of his flesh, this gives Thor's body a metallic or undead quality, or, more accurately, a sculptural character, which is typical of Fuseli's treatment of his most heroic heroes (fig.44). The impenetrable, armoured surfaces that characterise these heroes convey a sense of rectitude that conforms to prevalent sexual stereotypes (summed up in Fuseli's statement 'The forms of virtue are erect, the forms of pleasure undulate.')[4] The serpent and the sea are characterised in a quite different fashion. There are no clear linear boundaries to its form, and where the serpent's body coils up over itself thick slabs of paint cross over and intersect on the picture's surface, in defiance of the logic of the pictorial space. Where Thor's body is crisply delineated and cleanly painted, the serpent's form is furiously expressed in murky blacks and greys. This contrast in effect provides an idiosyncratic commentary on the customary opposition between two ways of painting – the precise, dry method identified with Renaissance Rome and Florence, and the richly painterly mode identified with Venetian and Flemish art. In the writings on art that he was beginning to formulate at this time, Fuseli was greatly concerned with what he perceived as the threat to modern art presented by the taste for richly painted pictures. Paint and colour themselves could destroy the work of art: 'when equally it overwhelms the forms of infancy, the milky germ of life, and the defined lines of manhood and beauty with lumpy pulp; when the dresser of the graces it becomes the handmaid of deformity, and with their spoils decks her limbs –

44 *Theseus Receiving
the Thread from
Ariadne* 1788
Oil on canvas
96 × 73
(37¾ × 28¾)
Kunsthaus Zurich

shakes hands with meanness, or haunts the recesses of loathsomeness and horror'.[5]

For Fuseli, the 'vile crust' formed by an over-painterly surface is disgusting and dangerous (even when the colours are enticing), as his comments on the exemplary artist of the Flemish school Rubens make abundantly clear: 'His male forms, generally the brawny pulp of slaughtermen; his females, hillock of roses in overwhelmed muscles, grotesque attitudes, and distorted joints, are swept along in a gulph of colours, as herbiage, trees and shrubs are whirled, tossed, and absorbed by inundation.'[6]

By these analogies, paint as raw matter is presented as physically threatening. Fuseli himself could be, and regularly was, accused of distortion and of creating grotesques, and his colouring even more often damned for 'loathsomeness and horror'. But on the terms of his arguments, these distortions and horrors were at least kept within the bounds (quite literally) of an emphatically linear way of painting, where outlines and muscles and joints are on the whole sharply marked, and where the physical surface of the paint is restrained. The much greater horror, according to his reasoning, would be where the artist is seduced by painterly colour, by the feel and sensuousness of paint itself, at the cost of marking form and outline.

These were not in themselves new arguments; high-minded writers on art in the eighteenth century often asserted the intellectual and moral supremacy of the more linear ways of painting over the seductive and immoral qualities of the painterly art that was meant to dominate in cultures organised around commerce. But Fuseli took this argument to a visceral extreme, acutely aware of the very real threats to the ideals of high art presented by consumer culture and political upheaval. With that in mind, we can argue that Thor's body is presented as an exaggeratedly masculine form not only in its physique, but in the very way it is painted. The painting visualises a sublime struggle between the hero and base matter as represented by the serpent. One contemporary even claimed that the very word 'sublime' was 'derived from *supra* and *limus*; and so denotes literally the circumstance of being raised *above* the *slime*, the *mud*, or the *mould*, of this world'.[7] Thor is legible as a sublime hero because he is literally raised above the monstrous and muddy form beneath him, and Fuseli is presented as a heroic painter because he shows himself to have extracted a figure of sculptural purity out of the mess of paint. *Thor Battering the Midgard Serpent* is a painting that comments upon the act of painting itself to underscore its claims about the nature of heroism.

Considered as a work intended to be exemplary of Academic standards of art, Fuseli's Diploma work is an oddity. However, as we have already seen, the very individuality of his work suited the emerging definitions of modern art in Britain, which stressed its vital diversity. The 1790s saw that definition clarified, through the combined force of rising nationalism and commercial initiative. The catalyst for this was the establishment of a series of galleries set up by entrepreneurs. The first and probably most important of these was the Shakespeare Gallery, initiated by the print publisher John Boydell in 1786 and opened in 1789. This was joined by similar schemes for paintings from British poetry by Thomas Macklin, a second Shakespeare gallery set up by James Woodmason, and galleries dedicated to the Bible and David Hume's *History of England* instituted by Macklin and Robert Bowyer. All these schemes were established on a similar plan; the entrepreneur would commission a series of pictures from modern artists on given subjects, make sure there was plenty of press coverage and bring the pictures together in a specially hired gallery open to the public. The interest this would raise would then, it was hoped, encourage people to buy the prints reproducing the pictures published by the entrepreneur. Almost every major painter of the period worked on one or more of these schemes, including Reynolds, West and Hamilton. Fuseli was involved in all these projects, producing some of the grandest canvases of his career for them.

For some of the artists involved, this was virtually the only chance they ever had to create history paintings for profit. James Barry, an Irish artist

45 James Barry
King Lear Weeping Over the Body of Cordelia 1786–7
Oil on canvas
269 × 367
(106 × 144½)
Tate

46 Robert Thew after Henry Fuseli
Hamlet, Horatio, Marcellus and the Ghost 1796
Stipple engraving
44.1 × 59.6
(17⅜ × 23½)
The British Museum

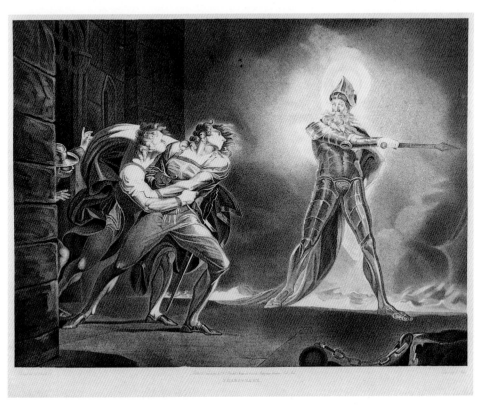

notorious for his stern conception of high art and his controversial opinions (he is the only painter ever to be expelled from the Royal Academy), painted his huge *King Lear Weeping over the Body of Cordelia* (fig.45) for Boydell – when all but a handful of his history paintings remained in his studio until his death. Fuseli, as might be expected, was most often asked to produce pictures on themes of high drama, fantasy and the supernatural, such as his sparsely conceived scene of Hamlet encountering his father's ghost (fig.46). His large paintings of *A Midsummer Night's Dream* executed for Boydell are among his most accomplished paintings, combining technical virtuosity, a hugely elaborate conception of Shakespeare's fairies, and his more personal concern with the minutiae of insect life (Fuseli was a keen amateur entomologist) (figs.47, 48). The very effusiveness of the *Midsummer Night's Dream* pictures suggests that Fuseli was pulling out all the stops. In the high-profile setting of the Shakespeare Gallery, there was perhaps even more pressure than in the Academy for each painter to outperform the next. If Fuseli was asked to paint some fairies, he was going to paint as many and various fairies as he could possibly conceive, and simply cram them into the canvas. If he was asked to paint Hamlet and the ghost, it would be the most ghostly ghost and the most energetic Hamlet imaginable. Fuseli's pictures for the commercial galleries show Fuseli being the most 'Fuselian' he ever was.

47 *Titania's Awakening* 1785–9
Oil on canvas
222 × 280
(87⅜ × 110¼)
Kunstmuseum, Winterthur

Given the source matter for the images, and the wide range of artists involved, it is no surprise that the pictures produced for the galleries varied greatly in terms of their character (and, it must be said, quality). But what was very generally agreed on was that this was a good thing. In later years, John Boydell reflected on the achievements of his Gallery:

> I might ... defy any of the Italian, Flemish, or French Schools, to show, in so short a space of time, such an exertion as the Shakespeare Gallery; and if they could have made such an exertion in so short a period, the pictures would have been marked with all that monotonous sameness which distinguishes these different Schools. Whereas, in the Shakespeare Gallery, every Artist, partaking of the freedom of his country, and endowed with that originality of thinking, so peculiar to its natives, has chosen his own road, to what he conceived to be excellence, unshackled by the slavish imitation and uniformity that pervade all the foreign schools.[8]

48 *Titania and Bottom* c.1790
Oil on canvas
217 × 276
(85½ × 108⅔)
Tate

What Boydell does here is to borrow the idea that the distinctive genius of English literature (exemplified by Shakespeare) lay in its variety and eccentricity and apply it to the British School of painting as a whole. This had a very strong patriotic and political aspect. The French Revolution, war and the threat of

political unrest at home led to a growing conservatism, and the desire to identify some kind of national cultural tradition despite the evident failings of the British state or ruling class to encourage public art. It was well established that the rules and regulations of classical and Continental literature did not restrict Shakespeare. Rather, his work was endowed with a degree of liberty. In the 1790s the political implications of such a view were explored to the full. The alliance of literary criticism and political re-entrenchment was summed up by Edmund Burke, the prime theorist of political conservatism, in a letter to the Shakespeare scholar Edmund Malone: 'Your admiration of Shakespeare would be ill sorted indeed, if your Taste (to talk of nothing else) did not lead you to a perfect abhorrence of the French Revolution, and all its works.'[9] The dominant critical view of the Shakespeare Gallery and its like was that they embodied an ideal of a diversified and libertarian national genius sustained by democratic political principles. If you loved Britain, then you would love Shakespeare and the poets, and love the rich diversity of modern British art, despite, or rather because of, all its failings. Visiting the Shakespeare Gallery was perhaps not simply a matter of consumer choice, in that case, but an expression of the true freedoms enjoyed only by patriotic Britons. In that context, Fuseli's ghosts and fairies were manifestations of individuality and emblems of national liberty (with the fact that Fuseli was born a foreigner but chose to work in Britain perhaps only making the point more firmly). Of course, what was really going on was commercial enterprise; ultimately, Boydell and his like wanted these visitors to buy the prints. Then, as now, in the right circumstances patriotism could be a great marketing device.

Seeing the success of these galleries, as early as 1790 Fuseli had decided 'to lay, hatch and Crack an egg *for myself*'.[10] The scheme he conceived was to create his own gallery of paintings based on the works of the seventeenth-century poet John Milton, which would form the basis of illustrations to a new and lavish edition of his works published by Joseph Johnson and edited by William Cowper. Widely considered as Britain's greatest epic poet, Milton would, it was hoped, serve Fuseli in his own claims to grandeur, offering a wide range of potential subject-matter, from the 'Sublime and Pathetic' to the 'Whimsical and phantastic'.[11] Although the original plan to publish an illustrated edition of Milton collapsed with the decline of Cowper's mental health, Fuseli was preoccupied with his work on the pictures for the proposed Milton Gallery throughout the 1790s, even failing to exhibit at the Academy for several years, though as an Academician his works were guaranteed a good position in the display. During this period he received essential financial support from a number of well-off friends, most notably the lawyer William Roscoe, the banker Thomas Coutts, the writers William Seward and George Steevens, and the wealthy amateur artist and Fuseli acolyte William Lock. Typically, these were professionals or men of letters, and Fuseli's high-minded ambition in the Milton Gallery reflected and extended their own cultural aspirations. What he produced with their support was a series of some forty or so canvases. Some of these were enormous works, on a par with the paintings he produced for Boydell. In subject and theme these range from the 'Sublime' *Sin, Pursued by Death* (fig.49) through sweetly conceived scenes of Milton's boyhood (based on his

Lycidas), the overwrought physical drama of the naked Adam and Eve, and the 'phantastic' of *The Shepherd's Dream* (fig.50). Reviewing the surviving images, one gets a sense of tumultuous visual drama, as gigantic figures lurch, fly and fight in a fantastical arena of suffocating blackness relieved only by storm clouds and rocky precipices. The pessimism can be overbearing: Fuseli's interpretation of *Paradise Lost*, which extended over thirty canvases, presents a vision of intensely physical conflict, with the rebellious Satan the vigorous hero of the piece, and no real hope of salvation. In theory, the Milton Gallery should have been Fuseli's greatest moment, the fullest expression of his aim to be a painter of an expansive pictorial scheme, in line with Raphael and Michelangelo. As the diarist Joseph Farington reported: 'On this Exhibition he totally depends, should it fail all is over with Him.'[12]

The Gallery finally opened in hired rooms in Pall Mall in May 1799, with forty pictures by Fuseli. It was immediately clear that it was a non-starter. The reports of people who went to the Gallery show that it was very sparsely attended. By June he had made £117 from entrance fees and the sale of catalogues, but in July 1799 the gallery had still only taken £170. Although he

49 Sin, Pursued by Death 1794–6
Oil on canvas
119 × 132
(46⅞ × 52)
Kunsthaus Zurich

tried to get the Gallery 'puffed' in the newspapers, things still did not improve and he was forced to close it down. Such was the worry the Gallery had caused him that he admitted to taking opium to help him relax.[13] The Gallery opened again in the spring of 1800 with the addition of seven more pictures. Despite a special dinner held by the Academy to support it, the Gallery again failed to raise public interest. The Milton Gallery had been an almost complete flop.

The failure of the Gallery can be explained in a number of ways. The wars against France prevented the export of prints to Europe, an important market for British publishers. This hit Bodyell and the other entrepreneurs very badly. It would not, though, explain the public's lack of interest in the exhibition itself. Partly, this may reflect the ambivalent status of Milton. The poet's association with republicanism made him politically suspect, and Fuseli himself was sometimes suspected of political dissidence, despite being openly critical of the later stages of the French Revolution. With the heightened nervousness about revolutionary tendencies in the 1790s, Fuseli was rightly upset that William Godwin had 'made a malevolent insinuation against his principles' in his *Life of Mary Wollstonecraft* (1798).[14] More than anything, perhaps, the plan single-handedly to produce a gallery of some forty pictures was simply a bad idea. The other commercial galleries were marketed on the basis of the diversity and range of works on show, reflecting patriotic arguments about modern British art, and embodying the law of consumer choice. Forty or more canvases painted by a single artist (with a single-minded sense of pessimism)

50 *The Shepherd's Dream* 1793
Oil on canvas
154 × 215
(60⅝ × 84⅝)
Tate

simply could not have the same sort of appeal. The Gallery did not become the 'fashionable Rage' it needed to be, as Farington saw when he told Fuseli he should 'get some ladies to attend his Exhibition to make it more general'.[15]

Despite his rather dramatic claims about the make-or-break significance of the Gallery, in many ways this was the period during which Fuseli settled down and achieved his greatest fame. His literary aspirations continued with his involvement in the highbrow journal *The Analytical Review*, his work on the English translation of Lavater's *Physiognomical Fragments*, and his advisory role on William Cowper's translation of Homer. In 1799, he was elected as Professor of Painting at the Royal Academy, securing him high status in the art community and a regular source of income, and in the event, some of the major pictures in the Milton Gallery were sold off to some very illustrious personages, including the fabulously wealthy art patron John Julius Angerstein and the Countess of Guilford. Following on from his prestigious work for the major commercial galleries, Fuseli became well established as an illustrator for smaller-scale literary publications, including a series of designs for an edition of Milton's *Paradise Lost*, that echo, if only in a diminutive form, his original plans for the Milton Gallery (fig.51). And having withdrawn himself from the print market in the 1790s, in 1802 he took the engraver Moses Haughton into his house and began publishing his own prints. All in all, Fuseli's reputation reached a peak. The exhibitions and prints, and the ever-expanding body of art criticism, put him in the position of Britain's leading artist of literary subjects. He was still viewed as a mannerist and an oddity, but that, perhaps, only demonstrated the healthy variety of the British art scene. The heroic individuality expressed in Fuseli's figure of Thor was often transferred onto the persona of Fuseli himself. Remembering a visit to Fuseli's house in 1805, Benjamin Robert Haydon wrote:

> I followed her [the maid] into a gallery or showroom, enough to frighten anybody at twilight. Galvanised devils – malicious witches brewing their incantations. – Satan bridging Chaos, and springing upwards like a pyramid of fire – Lady Macbeth – Paolo and Francesca – Falstaff and Mrs Quickly – humour, pathos, terror, blood, and murder met one at every look! I expected the floor to give way – I fancied Fuseli himself to be a giant.[16]

Haydon was then a young man new to London and full of hope about pursuing a career as a history painter. Fuseli, the painter of the heroic and terrible, whose works he knew from the papers and from prints, was his model of an artist. But then, Haydon continued, Fuseli himself appeared: 'I heard his footsteps and saw a little bony hand round the edge of the door, followed by a little white-headed lion-faced old man in an old flannel dressing-gown, tied round his waist with a piece of rope, and upon his head the bottom of Mrs Fuseli's work-basket.'

As the youthful Haydon witnessed, Fuseli's art was sensationalist and various, encompassing fear and loathing, humour and horror, Shakespeare, Milton and Dante. But Haydon, like Sergel in his earlier caricature (fig.17) plays with the comic contrast between the inflated reputation of the artist, now expanded by three decades of continuous press coverage and gossip, and Fuseli's diminutive figure in actuality. Fuseli's art, as it was puffed by his supporters, promised an heroic grandeur that was meant to reflect on the artist himself. But behind all the grandiose canvases stood a rather small, rather dishevelled old Swiss man – a Wizard of Oz figure. Seen in this light, Fuseli's art reflected both a patriotic ideal of the heroic individualism of British culture, and the very workings of the commerce in art that made painting a popular spectacle that promised more than it delivered.

Awake, arise, or be for ever fall'n!

51 William Bromley after Henry Fuseli *Satan Calling up his Legions* 1802 Engraving from *Milton's Paradise Lost* (London 1802) 11.6 × 9 (4½ × 3½) Birmingham Museums & Art Gallery

4

'THE DARK CHAMBERS
OF THE MIND'

Fuseli continued to exhibit at the Royal Academy until the year of his death. Although the most intensively productive period of his life was over, scenes from Shakespeare, Milton, the classics and modern and ancient poetry continued to appear most years at Somerset House. It would be difficult to claim any great innovation in his art from this period, though the range of his literary sources widened still further. Paintings such as the *Lady Macbeth Seizing the Daggers* show the same dramatic use of gesture and schematic anatomy apparent in his drawings of the 1770s (fig.52). The press criticism from these later years is remarkably similar to that which first emerged in response to his painting a full half-century before. All the old themes reappear – that Fuseli is above all a painter of the imagination who cannot be assessed by the conventional rules of art, that his genius is a form of madness, that his depiction of the human body is extravagant and caricatured. If anything, the criticism grows occasionally fiercer, now taking in attacks on his foreignness ('*his* distortions and vagaries are German, and not English: they lie like a night-mare on the breast of our native art'[1]) and suggesting that his mismanagement of the rules of art was almost criminal in nature. With radicalism and popular unrest emerging as more forceful influences on British political life, and the entrenchment of patriotic conservatism, Fuseli's apparent assaults on the order of art perhaps looked more threatening than ever, even as his status as a leading British painter was consolidated. The Fuseli who was being criticised in the nineteenth century was no longer the eccentric outsider, but the very embodiment of the art establishment. As Professor of Painting he delivered a series of high-profile lectures, and as Keeper of the Academy from 1804 he held the responsibility for the basic training of all the students and the day-to-day running of the schools. Since he was a representative of officially ordained art, his work was naturally embroiled in the growing factionalism of the early nineteenth-century art world. The informal journalism of the newspapers was now joined by essays in fashionable magazines and literary journals, expanding the debate around art and revealing an increasing division between the desire of the mass of the public for entertainment, and the earnest demands of a self-elected intelligentsia. The proper character of the British School of painting was hotly debated, as new art institutions challenged the authority of the Royal Academy, and as the relative value of the different genres of art was reassessed.

Whether praised or censured, Fuseli was seen as a decisive influence on a whole generation of artists. Critics looked out for 'Fuseli-looking pictures'[2] in the exhibitions, testifying to the fact 'that artists of the next century will have a new style to criticise or imitate called the "Fusilesque"'.[3] There are a host of painters and illustrators that we could distinguish as (if only occasionally and superficially) purveyors of this 'Fusilesque' style, including Henry Howard, Thomas Lawrence, Richard Westall, Thomas Stothard and Benjamin Robert Haydon. Fuseli's art was, furthermore, a model for artists considered as equally original, notably the sculptor John Flaxman and, most famously, William Blake. The relationship between Blake and Fuseli was a complex one. They were friends since at least 1787, and though Fuseli seems to have viewed the younger artist with some suspicion, they developed a close relationship of mutual respect. Blake was quite frequently employed to engrave reproductions of Fuseli's designs, and Fuseli wrote introductions for a number of publications illustrated by Blake. While Blake's deeply felt spiritual optimism was anathema to the sceptical Fuseli, his visionary art was nonetheless founded upon the Swiss painter's anti-naturalistic style (fig.53). Yet the small scale and often bafflingly personal iconography of Blake's work also flags up how far this heroic style was detached from its original intention as the basis of a grandly public art. Blake set out to be a history painter working on a large scale, but facing the prevailing lack of interest among the public and patrons for such works, found alternative means of expression in creating illuminated books

52 *Lady Macbeth Seizing the Daggers*
1812
Oil on canvas
101.6 × 127
(40 × 50)
Tate

53 William Blake
*The Good and Evil
Angels* 1795/1805
Colour print finished
in ink and
watercolour
44.5 × 59.4
(17½ × 23⅜)
Tate

and generally tiny paintings that had an incredibly small audience originally. However we may value Blake's creations now, we should also realise that they represent Fuseli's heroic style being reduced and made obscure almost to the point of no return. His reward was being the only artist of the period considered even madder than Fuseli.

If Fuseli was demonstrably an artistic model for numerous practising artists, he was also, more literally, the teacher of a still younger generation. As Keeper of the Academy, it was Fuseli who administered the enrolment of new students, and taught in the Plaster Schools (where the students would draw from casts after antique sculptures) and life-drawing classes. It seems that Fuseli was much admired and liked by the students, to the extent that, in 1807, they presented him with a specially designed silver vase as a way of thanking him. But there are many reports of his unconventional teaching methods, which ranged from his ignoring the students outright to interfering very directly and rather unhelpfully by scratching out and reworking their drawings in front of them. One such recollection, from the American-born painter Charles Robert Leslie, is of special interest:

> I was now [1812] admitted a student in the Antique Academy of
> which Fuseli was the keeper. I had been impressed with the greatest
> respect for his genius, both as a painter and a writer, before I left
> America. The engraving from his 'Hamlet and the Ghost' [fig.46] had
> scared me from the window of a print shop in Philadelphia, and I still
> contemplate that matchless spectre with something of the same awe
> which it then inspired. I hoped for much advantage from studying
> under such a master, but he said little in the Academy. He generally
> came into the room once in the course of every evening, and rarely

without a book in his hand. He would take any vacant place among the students, and sit reading nearly the whole time he stayed with us. I believe he was right. For those students who are born with powers that will make them eminent, it is sufficient to place fine works of art before them. They do not want instruction, and those that do are not worth it. Art may be *learnt* but can't be *taught*. Under Fuseli's wise neglect, Wilkie, Mulready, Etty, Landseer, and Haydon distinguished themselves, and were the better for not being made all alike by teaching, if indeed that could have been done.[4]

As well as reminding us of the sheer geographical reach of Fuseli's fame through the medium of printed reproductions, this account claims his failure to teach conventionally as a decisive influence on the leading artists of the mid-nineteenth century. Certainly it would be hard to distinguish any attempt to emulate Fuseli in the naturalistic paintings of William Mulready, Edwin Landseer or David Wilkie (fig.54), and we might find only faint echoes of the artist in the fleshy subject-pictures of William Etty. But in so doing, Leslie testifies to the loss of faith in the Academic system of teaching art, that Fuseli himself expressed in his *Lectures on Painting*. Traditional art training, based on the careful study of antique models and an idealising way of representing the life model, was intended to prepare artists for the field of history painting. Yet, despite the brief flourishing of literary painting stimulated by the commercial galleries of the 1790s, history painting remained on the whole an unprofitable activity. Painting in general was, however, flourishing as it never had before, with portraiture, landscape and 'genre paintings' of ordinary life proving a means to unprecedented fame and fortune. Many writers on art saw these developments as the expression of a renewed British School of painting, that had all the poetry and power of history painting, without being tied to the old

54 David Wilkie
The Blind Fiddler
1806
Oil on mahogany
57.8 × 79.4
(22¾ × 31¼)
Tate

55 *Fairy Mab*
1815–20
Oil on canvas
70 × 90
(27½ × 35⅜)
The Folger
Shakespeare Library

56 Theodor von
Holst, *Bertelda
Frightened by
Apparitions* 1830–5
Oil on canvas
98.5 × 82
(38¾ × 32¼)
Cheltenham Art
Gallery & Museums,
Gloucestershire, UK

subjects and rules. The familiar arguments about the democratic individualism of British art were revived, now with a special emphasis on naturalism as
a distinguishing characteristic of the national school. The best and most
British of British artists looked at nature unmediated by art, it was claimed.
With that in mind, the old hierarchies of subject-matter and style seemed
antiquated to many people. By the end of his life, Fuseli was looking like a figure from a different era, which of course he was. He had set out on a career as
an artist in a period of high hopes, when Reynolds and West had promised a
new era of classical history painting in the mould of the Renaissance masters.
He lived into an era when David Wilkie's sentimental little pictures of ordinary
life were the greatest successes of the Academy exhibitions. A public for art
had emerged as a permanent and powerful force directing the way artists
worked, but that public generally preferred sensationalism or sentiment or
'realistic' pictures over high art, as it was traditionally defined.

The Fuseli who was remembered as the nineteenth century progressed
was an artist quite different from the one who saw himself as the heir to
Michelangelo. What was retained most productively was the memory of him
as a private fantasist. His pictures of ghosts and fairies, 'the hobgoblinry of the
Teutonic genius',[5] were imitated by Theodor von Holst (figs.55, 56), an artist
who was, in turn, greatly admired by Rossetti, forming a bridge between Fuseli
and the Pre-Raphaelites. For the Victorians, Fuseli's 'hobgoblinry' appeared
wilfully fanciful, fevered 'Romantic' outpourings, exotic and decadent. The
erotic aspect of his imagery was of singular importance. The artist's attitudes
to women may have been complex (while he damned 'clever women' he also
associated with them), but in his art female figures are cast along the stereotypical, misogynistic lines of being either whores or virgins. All in all, the
whores have the upper hand. The anxiety the artist felt personally about
the rise of women's power in a consumer society found ready expression in
the images of teasing viragos in many of his public works, such as the light-
hearted *Falstaff in the Buck Basket* exhibited in 1792 (fig.57). In contrast, *The
Nightmare* (fig.1) has been read as a revenge-fantasy directed at Anna Landolt,
the woman he had loved and been rejected by while on his visit to Switzerland
in 1779.[6] Here, the woman is reduced to a limp and lifeless, almost shapeless
form, virginal in her revealing white nightdress but yielding under the suffocating weight of the imp on her chest (whose features are sometimes said to
resemble the artist's). Women were a veritable obsession in his private drawings, where he paid enormous attention to the intricate details of hair and costume, his crisp linear rendering of their patterns itself conveying a sense of
erotic attention (figs.58, 59). Although this tendency has often been interpreted in primarily personal terms (even to the extent of identifying the great
majority of such images as portraits of his wife), we should also read them in
terms of a specifically male response to more general pressures and concerns
about shifting gender identities and the rise of women's power through consumerism as well as political and intellectual activity. This is true even of the
several groups of frankly pornographic scenes he executed, where lone male
figures are pleasured simultaneously from several angles, sodomised by a
woman with a strap-on dildo, or threatened with castration (fig.60). These

57 *Falstaff in the Buck Basket* 1792
Oil on canvas
137 × 170
(54 × 66⅞)
Kunsthaus Zurich

drawings can be interpreted as an imaginative working-through of the fears about women's authority experienced in Fuseli's time: women's real claims to power being translated into much simpler (and ultimately degrading) sexual hunger. These are drawings in the stylistic language of heroic art, made into a private fantasy where heroes and maidens are transformed into 'eunuchs' and 'viragos' – Michelangelo for the masturbator. Their explicit content may have made them unsuitable for consumption by the contemporary art audience, but in their draughtsmanship and repetitive arrangement and rearrangement of the human form they are little different from the straining heroes and heroines that appeared in Fuseli's public paintings. In both his public and his private art Fuseli reduced the struggle between the sexes to a visceral fantasy. But this was a fantasy that had the most lasting appeal. Despite what we must assume was their intensely private nature, Fuseli's most explicit drawings seem to have enjoyed some currency. His imitators Thomas Griffiths Wainewright and von Holst duplicated his distinctive treatment of the attenuated female form and elaborate costume in their own drawings. The latter drew a series of pornographic images, more or less copied from Fuseli, that apparently entered the collection of no less a personage than George IV (fig.61). Echoes of his fetishistic treatment of hair and necks, which gives the

58 *Half-length Figure
of a Courtesan with
Feathers, a Bow and a
Veil in her Hair*
1800–10
Pen, pencil and
watercolour
28.3 × 20
(11⅛ × 7⅞)
Kunsthaus Zurich

59 *The Debutante*
1807
Drawing and
watercolour
37.1 × 24.1
(14⅝ × 9½)
Tate

60 *Symplegma: A Man with Three Women c.*1809–10
Pencil drawing
18 × 24.5 (7⅛ × 9⅝)
The Victoria & Albert Museum

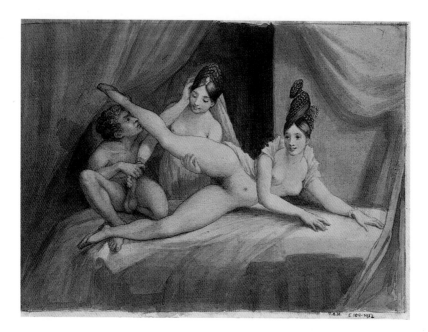

61 Theodor von Holst
*Ithyphallic Man and Two Women with Elaborate Hairstyles c.*1822–30
Pencil and watercolour
23 × 18.9 (9 × 7⅜)
The Victoria & Albert Museum

signs of elegant femininity a threateningly phallic quality, are even apparent in J.M.W. Turner's painted images of women (fig.62).

It was on the basis of the exotic and erotic aspects of his art that Fuseli was 'rediscovered' in the 1930s and 1940s. Then his art, most especially his drawings, represented something strange and personal, an unbounded exploration of 'the dark chambers of the mind'[7] that resonated in the days of psychoanalysis and of the real terrors of war. Fuseli is still best remembered as the painter of *The Nightmare*, a painting that continues to embody a powerful idea of Romantic eroticism and attracts rather self-referential psychoanalytic interpretations. To the non-specialist, his art must appeal mainly because of all the sex, violence and fantasy. But if we recover Fuseli only as a fantasist, an eccentric, or a 'Romantic designer before Romanticism',[8] we recover only one small part of the artist. Fuseli's art was a response to the emergence of a modern art world that we have inherited. His works are sensationalist, pretentious, stereotypical and sometimes fatuous, but also dynamic, memorable and adventurous. In all those respects, he was, perhaps, only the artist that our modern world of consumerism and spectacle deserved.

62 J.M.W. Turner
*Two Women with a Letter c.*1830
Oil on canvas
121.9 × 91.4
(48 × 36)
Tate

Notes

Introduction: 'Both Turk and Jew'

1 Ruthven Todd, *Tracks in the Snow*, London 1946, p.84.
2 John Barrell, *The Political Theory of Painting from Reynolds to Hazlitt*, New Haven and London 1986, pp.259–60.
3 David V. Erdman (ed.), *The Complete Poetry and Prose of William Blake*, New York 1982, p.507.

Chapter One: 'The Wild Painter'

1 6 May 1768, in Walter Muschg (ed.), *Heinrich Fuessli: Briefe*, Basel 1942, pp.143–4.
2 From a letter from Hume to Hugh Blair, 20 May 1767, in David H. Weinglass (ed.), *The Collected English Letters of Henry Fuseli*, Millwood, London and Nendeln 1982 (hereafter referred to as *Letters*).
3 From his own, anonymous, review of the *Remarks*, in Eudo C. Mason, *The Mind of Henry Fuseli*, London 1951, p.134.
4 On this circle, and their social activities, see Nancy L. Pressly, *The Fuseli Circle in Rome: Early Romantic Art of the 1770s*, exh. cat., Yale Center for British Art, New Haven 1979; Ulf Cederlöf, 'On an Unearthed Roman Group Portrait with Sergel, by Esprit Gibelin', in *Nationalmuseum Bulletin*, 3 (1979), pp.169–78; Jørgen, *De År I Rom: Abildgaard, Sergel, Füssli*, Copenhagen 1989.
5 John Cartwright to A. K. Dashwood, 12 May 1772, in *Letters*, p.13; Thomas Banks to Joseph Nollekens, 31 July 1773, in *Letters*, p.14; Lavater to Herder, 4 November 1773, Muschg, *Briefe*, p.168.
6 Letters of 4 February and 16 November 1774, translated in Mason, *Mind of Henry Fuseli*, p.67.
7 See Martin Bircher and Karl S. Guthke (eds.), *Johann Heinrich Füssli: Sämtliche Gedichte*, Zurich 1973, pp.67–8. The 'Second Ode on Art' has been translated by A.M. Atkins, '"Both Turk and Jew": Notes on the Poetry of Henry Fuseli, with Some Translations', *Blake: An Illustrated Quarterly*, Spring 1983, pp.206–11 (pp.209–10).
8 John Cartwright to A.K. Dashwood, 12 May 1772, in *Letters*, pp.13–14.
9 Thomas Banks to James Northcote, 31 July 1771, in *Letters*, p.14; letter from John Thorpe to the 8th Earl of Arundell, 4 June 1774 (Wiltshire County Record Office, Trowbridge, 2667/20 Box 3).
10 4 February 1774, Arnold Federmann, *Johann Heinrich Füssli: Dichter und Maler 1741–1825*, Zurich and Leipzig 1942, p.152.
11 Reported in Prince Hoare's 'Biographic Sketch of Henry Fuseli', *The Monthly Mirror*, vol.11 (January 1801), p.7.
12 Letter to Lavater, 14 June 1777, in Muschg, *Briefe*, pp.175–7.
13 See Alan Mansfield and Barbara McGinn, 'Pumping Irony: The Muscular and the Feminine' in Sue Scott and David Morgan (eds.), *Body Matters: Essays on the Sociology of the Body*, London and Washington 1993, pp.49–68, and Sam Fussell, 'Bodybuilder Americanus' in Laurence Goldstein (ed.), *The Male Body: Features, Destinies, Exposures*, Ann Arbor 1994, pp.43–60.
14 *London Chronicle*, 24–6 April 1777; *General Advertiser* clipping in the exhibition files, Witt Library, Courtauld Institute of Art, inscribed 'April 1777'.
15 Clipping in the exhibition files, Witt Library, Courtauld Institute of Art, inscribed 'April 1777'.

Chapter Two: 'Shockingly mad, madder than ever'

1 Letter of 28 September 1778, in *Letters*, p.18.
2 Sir Joshua Reynolds to Lord Grantham, 20 July 1773, in Jeremy Black and Nicholas Penny, 'Letters from Reynolds to Lord Grantham', in *Burlington Magazine* 124 (1987) pp.730–4.
3 British Library, Add. MSS 41,135, f.22v.
4 13 June 1783, British Library, Eg. MSS 1970, ff.139–139v.
5 Note in the Royal Academy Catalogue of 1783, in the Collection of the Dowager Countess Rosebery (photographic record in the Witt Library, Courtauld Institute of Art).
6 Henry Fuseli to Robert Smyth, 17 August 1780, in *Letters*, p.20.
7 Including: *Public Advertiser*, 3 May 1781; *London Courant*, 1 May 1781, 12 May 1781, 28 May 1781; *Morning Chronicle*, 5 May 1781; *Morning Herald*, 8 May 1781; *St James's Chronicle*, 28 April–1 May 1781; also, *The Ear-Wig: Or An Old Woman's Remarks on the Present Exhibition of Pictures*, London 1781, pp.7, 13.
8 See Horace Walpole to Horace Mann, 25 February 1782 (W.S. Lewis (ed.), *The Yale Edition of Horace Walpole's Correspondence*, 48 vols., Oxford and New Haven 1937–83, vol.25, p.247) and, quoted here, 8 September 1782 (vol.25, p.316) and Henry Fuseli to an unknown addressee, circa September 1783, in *Letters*, p.21.
9 From Fuseli's 'Aphorisms on Art', published in John Knowles, *The Life and Writings of Henry Fuseli*, 3 vols., London 1831, vol.III, p.94.
10 See Leslie A. Marchand (ed.), *Byron's Letters and Journals*, 12 vols., London 1973–82, vol.3, pp.233–4 (journal, 20 March 1814).
11 Letter of 22 October 1791, in *Letters*, p.74.
12 The following interpretation of the Gothic novel is especially indebted to Andrea K. Henderson, *Romantic Identities: Varieties of Subjectivity, 1774–1830*, Cambridge 1996.
13 Note in the Royal Academy Catalogue of 1785, in the Collection of the Dowager Countess Rosebery (photographic record in the Witt Library, Courtauld Institute of Art).

Photographic Credits

14 *Public Advertiser*, 31 May 1790; Kenneth Garlick *et al.* (eds.), *The Diary of Joseph Farington*, 17 vols., New Haven and London 1978–98, vol.3, p.660 (11 September 1796) and vol.4, p.1300 (7 November 1799); *Public Advertiser*, 2 May 1780, 1 May 1783.

15 Clipping dated 1790 in the exhibition files, Witt Library, Courtauld Institute of Art.

16 Samuel Northcote to James Northcote, 26 July 1789, in British Library, Add. MSS 47,792 (James Northcote's autobiography, vol.3), ff.36–36v.

17 On the bodily origins of 'taste' in the aesthetic sense see Terry Eagleton, *The Ideology of the Aesthetic*, Oxford 1990, pp.13–16.

18 From 'Press cuttings from English newspapers on matters of artistic interest, especially notices of exhibitions, sale-announcements etc., 1686–1835', vol.1, p.194, National Art Library, Victoria and Albert Museum.

Chapter Three: 'Humour, pathos, terror, blood'

1 Knowles, *Life and Writings of Henry Fuseli*, vol.3, p.144 (Aphorism 226).

2 A comment recorded by Mary Balmanno, *Pen and Pencil*, London 1858, p.204.

3 In that respect, these figures play the same role as the onlookers in the shoot-out scenes in modern Westerns. See Steve Neale, 'Masculinity as Spectacle: Reflections on Men and Mainstream Cinema', in *Screen*, 24:6 (1983), pp.2–16.

4 Knowles, *Life and Writings of Henry Fuseli*, vol.III, p.135.

5 Knowles, *Life and Writings of Henry Fuseli*, vol.II, pp.334–5.

6 Knowles, *Life and Writings of Henry Fuseli*, vol.II, p.369.

7 See James Beattie, *Dissertations Moral and Critical*, London 1783, p.606.

8 John Boydell to Sir John William Anderson, 4 February 1804, in 'Preface' (unpaginated), Collec-

tion of Prints, From Pictures Painted for the Purpose of Illustrating the Dramatic Works of Shakespeare, by the Artists of Great Britain, London 1803 ('Preface' dated 1805).

9 Edmund Burke to Edmund Malone, 5 April 1796, in Thomas W. Copeland (ed.), *The Correspondence of Edmund Burke*, 10 vols., Chicago 1958–78, vol.8, p.456.

10 Letter to William Roscoe, 17 August 1790, in *Letters*, p.61.

11 Letter to William Roscoe, 24 May 1799, in *Letters*, p.196.

12 *Diary of Joseph Farington*, vol.4, p.1145 (23 January 1799).

13 *Diary of Joseph Farington*, vol.4, p.1300 (7 November 1799).

14 *Diary of Joseph Farington*, vol.3, p.1043 (3 August 1798).

15 *Diary of Joseph Farington*, vol.4, p.1226 (20 May 1799).

16 Malcolm Elwin (ed.), *The Autobiography and Journals of Benjamin Robert Haydon*, London 1950, p.25.

Chapter Four: 'The dark chambers of the mind'

1 *Edinburgh Review*, August 1820, p.107.

2 *The Literary Gazette*, 1819, p.378.

3 James Dallaway, *Anecdotes of the Arts in England*, London 1800, p.524.

4 Tom Taylor (ed.), *Autobiographical Recollections of Charles Robert Leslie*, 2 vols., London 1860, vol.1, p.37.

5 Sidney Colvin, 'Henry Fuseli', in *The Portfolio* (1873), pp.50–6 (p.53).

6 For the reputation of this picture see Nicolas Powell, *Fuseli: The Nightmare*, London 1973.

7 Sacheverell Sitwell, *Splendours and Miseries*, London 1943, p.223.

8 Colvin, in *The Portfolio* (1873), p.56.

Birmingham Museums & Art Gallery 18, 51
The British Library 5, 6, 39
The British Museum 8, 24, 38, 41, 46
Cheltenham Art Gallery & Museums, Gloucestershire, UK/Bridgeman Art Library 56
The Courtauld Institute Gallery, London 13, 15
© 1997 The Detroit Institute of Arts 1
The Folger Shakespeare Library 55
© 2000 Kunsthaus Zurich. All rights reserved 2, 4, 7, 11, 12, 25, 26, 27, 28, 34, 35, 43, 44, 49, 57, 58
Kunstmuseum, Winterthur 47
National Galleries of Scotland Picture Library 9, 14
© Board of Trustees, National Gallery of Art, Washington 22
The National Museum of Fine Arts, Stockholm 3, 17, 21
Board of Trustees of the National Museums and Galleries on Merseyside (Walker Art Gallery, Liverpool) 19
National Museum of Western Art, Tokyo 32
By courtesy of the National Portrait Gallery, London 16
Öffentliche Kunstsammlung Basel, Martin Bühler 23
Royal Academy of Arts, London 42
Royal Academy of Arts, London/Prudence Cuming Associates Limited 29
The Royal Collection © 2000, Her Majesty Queen Elizabeth II / Photographic Records 30
Sir John Soane's Museum 36
© Spencer House/Mark Fiennes 33
Swarthmore College, Swarthmore, Pennsylvania 20
Tate Photography 10, 37, 45, 48, 50, 52, 53, 54, 59, 62
V&A Picture Library 60, 61
Yale Center for British Art, Paul Mellon Collection, USA/Bridgeman Art Library 31, 40

Chronology

1741 Born, Zurich, Switzerland, 6 February. Son of Johann Caspar Füssli, painter, art historian and civic official, and Elisabeth (née Waser).

1758/9–61 Studies theology at Caroline College in Zurich. Taught by the philosophers Bodmer and Breitinger, and befriends Johann Caspar Lavater.

1762 With Lavater publishes a pamphlet attacking the corruption of the magistrate Grebel. They are advised to leave Zurich.

1763 End of the Seven Years War. Travels in Germany, meeting many famous men of letters.

1764 Travels to London with Sir Andrew Mitchell, English ambassador in Berlin. Mitchell introduces Fuseli to literary society.

1765 Publishes his English translation of Winckelmann's *Reflections on the Painting and Sculpture of the Greeks*.

1766 Travels to Paris as tutor to the 14-year-old Lord Chewton and meets the philosopher Jean Jacques Rousseau. The appointment is terminated after a furious row in September.

1767–9 Returning to London from Paris, takes up his literary career again with essays and reviews. Publishes *Remarks on the Writings and Conduct of J.J. Rousseau* (1767). Meets Reynolds, who encourages him to paint. Foundation of the Royal Academy (December 1768).

1770 A fire at Johnson's house destroys Fuseli's possessions, including all his literary manuscripts. Backed by the banker Thomas Coutts and other sources, travels to Italy in the spring.

1770–8 In Italy. Based in Rome, making brief visits to Venice, Naples and Turin.

1778 Leaves Rome, travels through northern Italy and stays in Switzerland, where he paints portraits and begins work on *The Oath of the Ruttli* for Zurich Town Hall.

1779 Returns to London.

1780 Somerset House opens, with a suite of rooms and galleries for the Royal Academy. Begins to exhibit regularly.

1782 Exhibits *The Nightmare* at the Academy. Meets William Roscoe, a Liverpool-based lawyer. Roscoe to be his most constant patron.

1786 Invited to contribute paintings to John Boydell's Shakespeare Gallery.

1788 Macklin's Poet's Gallery opens. Begins publishing essays and reviews for the highbrow *Analytical Review*. Publishes translation of Lavater's *Aphorisms on Man* and announces publication of his own *Aphorisms on Art*, which, however, remain unpublished at his death. Marries Sophia Rawlins (30 July) and is elected Associate Member of the Royal Academy (3 November).

1789 The French Revolution begins; like many in Britain at this date, Fuseli welcomes it as a sign of 'an age pregnant with the most gigantic efforts of character'. Shakespeare Gallery opens in Pall Mall.

1790 Elected Full Member of the Royal Academy (10 December). Begins plans for his Milton Gallery.

1791 Issues proposals for publishing thirty prints based on his Milton pictures.

1793 In France, Louis XVI is executed by revolutionaries. Fuseli follows general opinion in condemning the revolution as despotic and anarchic. Britain declares war on France.

1799 Milton Gallery opens, with 40 paintings by Fuseli, to almost complete public indifference. Elected Professor of Painting at the Academy (29 June). Milton Gallery closes prematurely in July.

1800 Milton Gallery reopens briefly, with seven additional pictures.

1801 Publishes first three *Lectures on Painting*.

1802 Temporary peace between Britain and France; Fuseli, and many other artists, visit Paris.

1804 Elected Keeper of the Royal Academy (24 December); subsequently resigns as Professor of Painting.

1809 Re-elected Professor of Painting while retaining post of Keeper.

1815 Napoleon defeated at Waterloo, ending war with France.

1816 Following a visit to England by Antonia Canova, Fuseli is elected a member of the Academy of St Luke in Rome.

1825 16 April, dies at the Countess of Guilford's country residence at Putney Hill. 25 April, buried in St Paul's Cathedral, next to Sir Joshua Reynolds.

Select Bibliography

Henry Fuseli and his circle

Antal, Frederick, *Fuseli Studies*, London 1956.

Bircher, Martin and Guthke, Karl S. (eds.), *Johann Heinrich Füssli: Sämtliche Gedichte*, Zurich 1973.

Browne, Max, *The Romantic Art of Theodor von Holst 1810–44*, London 1994.

Hall, Carol Louise, *Blake and Fuseli: A Study in the Transmission of Ideas*, New York and London 1985.

Mason, Eudo C., *The Mind of Henry Fuseli*, London 1951.

Muschg, Walter (ed.), *Heinrich Fuessli: Briefe*, Basel 1942.

Pressly, Nancy L., *The Fuseli Circle in Rome: Early Romantic Art of the 1770s*, Yale Center for British Art, New Haven 1979.

Schiff, Gert, *Johann Heinrich Füssli*, 2 vols., Zurich and Munich 1973.

Schiff, Gert, *Henry Fuseli 1741–1825*, Tate Gallery, London 1975.

Tomory, Peter, *The Life and Art of Henry Fuseli*, London 1972.

Walker, John, 'Maria Cosway, an Undervalued Artist', in *Apollo*, 123 (1986), pp.318–24.

Weinglass, David H. (ed.), *The Collected English Letters of Henry Fuseli*, Millwood, London and Nendeln 1982.

Weinglass, David H., *Prints and Engraved Illustrations by and after Henry Fuseli: A Catalogue Raisonné*, Aldershot 1994.

Art and culture in Fuseli's time

Barrell, John, *The Political Theory of Painting from Reynolds to Hazlitt*, New Haven and London 1986.

Boime, Albert, *Art in an Age of Revolution 1750–1800*, Chicago and London 1987.

Bätschmann, Oskar, *The Artist in the Modern World: The Conflict Between Market and Self-Expression*, Cologne 1997.

Brewer, John, *Pleasures of the Imagination: English Culture in the Eighteenth Century*, London 1997.

Eaves, Morris, *The Counter-Arts Conspiracy: Art and Industry in the Age of Blake*, Ithaca and London 1992.

Klancher, Jon P., *The Making of English Reading Audiences 1790–1832*, Wisconsin 1987.

Kriz, Kay Dian, *The Idea of the English Landscape Painter: Genius as Alibi in the Early Nineteenth Century*, New Haven and London 1997.

McKendrick, Neil, Brewer, John and Plumb, J.H., *The Birth of a Consumer Society: The Commercialisation of Eighteenth-Century England*, London 1982.

Solkin, David H., *Painting for Money: The Visual Arts and the Public Sphere in Eighteenth-Century England*, New Haven and London 1993.

Genius, Gothic and the Sublime

de Bolla, Peter, *The Discourse of the Sublime: Readings in History, Aesthetics and the Subject*, Oxford 1989.

Clery, E.J., *The Rise of Supernatural Fiction, 1762–1800*, Cambridge 1995.

Ferguson, Frances, *Solitude and the Sublime: Romanticism and the Aesthetics of Individuation*, New York and London 1992.

Henderson, Andrea K., *Romantic Identities: Varieties of Subjectivity, 1774–1830*, Cambridge 1996.

Index